Queens
and Revolutionaries

Queens
and Revolutionaries

New Readings of Jean Genet

Pascale Gaitet

DELAWARE

Newark: University of Delaware Press
London: Associated University Presses

Associated University Presses
2010 Eastpark Boulevard
Cranbury, NJ 08512

Associated University Presses
Unit 304, The Chandlery
50 Westminster Bridge Road
London SE1 7QY, England

Associated University Presses
P.O. Box 338, Port Credit
Mississauga, Ontario
Canada L5G 4L8

The paper used in this publication meets the requirements of the American National Standard for Permanence of Paper for Printed Library Materials Z39.48–1984.

Library of Congress Cataloging-in-Publication Data

Gaitet, Pascale.
 Queens and revolutionaries : new readings of Jean Genet / Pascale Gaitet.
    p. cm.
Includes bibliographical references and index.
 ISBN 0-87413-826-4 (alk. paper)
1. Genet, Jean, 1910—Criticism and interpretation. 2. Transvestites in literature. 3. Homosexuality in literature. 4. Revolutionaries in literature. I. Title.

PQ2613.E53 Z66 2003
848'.91209—dc21

2002152994

PRINTED IN THE UNITED STATES OF AMERICA

Contents

Acknowledgments

I wish to thank my colleagues Helene Moglen, Suzanne Nash, Katherine Stern and Gerry Prince who generously spared time from their own work to read the manuscript and offer valuable help and encouragement. In addition, I am very much indebted to Cheryl Van De Veer who, with great skill and patience, proofread the text, formatted the manuscript and provided crucial editorial guidance. I wish also to acknowledge the assistance provided by the Committee on Research of the University of California, Santa Cruz.

Abbreviations

Works frequently cited have been identified using the following abbreviations:

ED:	*L'Ennemi déclaré*
F:	*"Fragments"*
FR:	*Funeral Rites*
OLF:	*Our Lady of the Flowers*
PL:	*Prisoner of Love*
Q:	*Querelle*
SG:	*Saint Genet*
TJ:	*The Thief's Journal*
*	my translation
mod:	translation modified

Queens
and Revolutionaries

Introduction

BEFORE ADDRESSING THE SUBJECT OF THIS BOOK, I SHOULD SAY A FEW words about the trajectory that brought me to it and situate it in relation to my past work. My first book, *Political Stylistics*, is a study of the representation of argot and popular language in canonical French novels of the nineteenth and twentieth centuries.[1] The idea of studying the movement by which popular speech is displaced from social margin to literary center occurred to me while I was an undergraduate at Oxford and found myself intrigued by certain upper class young men who chose to adopt (in their manner of clothing, their professed cultural tastes, their diction) a punk style: a style that originated among poor, unemployed youth in large industrial cities of Northern England. The reasons for this appropriation, the very specific modalities of its aesthetics and the effects of its reception interested me and led me to study a similar phenomenon in the literary realm. My work on Genet initially stems from a similar observation, from my interest in another type of stylistic displacement: the appropriation and performance of the feminine by gay men. As were my punk Oxford graduate friends for my first book, queens I've known are at the origin of my work on Genet.

In light of this, and transferring the male appropriation of the feminine into the realm of literature, my initial intention had been to consider Genet's texts as examples of *écriture féminine* [feminine writing], taking as a theoretical point of departure a remark by Hélène Cixous in "The Laugh of the Medusa": in a provocative footnote, she cites Genet, along with Colette and Duras, as examples of such a writing.[2] While it is true that a number of features of Genet's texts, most notably the celebration of the phallus, appear highly incompatible

13

with this notion, there are certainly ways in which they conform to what Cixous describes in that essay and elsewhere. I will briefly comment on these features here, for they do inform my later approach to Genet. One characteristic of such a writing is stylistic: the language of *écriture féminine* is one that disrupts grammatical rules, creating ambiguous, multiple meanings and destabilizing the signifying process. It is indeed the case that Genet's prose constantly draws on poetic processes—rhythm, alliteration, assonance, dissonance—and its finely wrought syntax produces semantic ambiguities. This process of defamiliarization operates not only on the level of the sentence but on a larger structural framework as well: the nonlinear time scale of *Our Lady of the Flowers* immediately comes to mind (the narrative plunges unexpectedly back into Louis/Divine's childhood, weaves its way in and out of the narrator's prison cell, in and out of fantasy) and so do unannounced changes of narrative voice in *Funeral Rites*.[3] Such a style —pliant, wrought, complex—participates in a vital function of *écriture féminine:* the undoing of binary oppositions. And, indeed, Genet's texts are pervaded by such undoings, as he himself acknowledges in the opening pages of *A Thief's Journal:* one of his goals is "to negate fundamental oppositions."[4] This occurs of course linguistically, through the process of defamiliarization I mentioned above, and structurally, through the merging of past and present, reality and fantasy. Such a fusion sometimes occurs in the aesthetics that Genet advocates ("To achieve harmony in bad taste is the height of elegance" [*TJ*, 120]) and in the imagery that springs from the fusion of opposites—but unlike surrealism, not randomly. Some of the most powerful aspects of Genet's work are the tortuous and delicate connections he makes and that end with conclusions such as "There is a close relationship between flowers and convicts" (*TJ*, 9).

Genet undoes oppositions on a thematic level also, most notably in the sexual realm, where, for example, active/passive dichotomies are blurred. This is important; unlike for instance Julia Kristeva's semiotic writing, the specificity of *écriture féminine* does not lie in the style and structure of a text alone (if that were the case, one could argue that a great number of modernist texts would qualify as such). Cixous explains that feminine writing involves a decipherable libidinal femininity which can be read in a writing produced by a male or a female.[5]

One of the characteristics of this libidinal femininity is what Cixous calls "the other bisexuality" and which is defined as each one's location in self of the presence—variously manifest and insistent according to each person, male or female, of both sexes, non-exclusion either of the difference or of one sex, and from this "self permission" multiplication of the effects of the inscription of desire, over all parts of my body and the other body.[6]

There are ways in which Genet's characters bring to literary life this "other bisexuality" (which opposes neutrality, androgyny) as masculine and feminine styles (constituted by words, gestures, voices) freely circulate across bodies. In *The Thief's Journal*, Armand, usually the toughest of the tough, described as a "perfect brute," is, on occasion, a lacemaker; Darling, of *Our Lady of the Flowers*, even though he carries himself most of the time with "the weighty magnificence of the barbarian who tramples choice furs beneath his muddy boots" might, on occasion, "strangle himself with his lithe arm, the arm of a tragedienne" (*OLF*, 59 and 61).

Shortly after I began seriously thinking about this study, a collection of Genet's essays, *L'Ennemi déclaré*, was published in France.[7] They rekindled my curiosity about Genet's relationship to the political—an interest originally sparked by my reading of his *Prisoner of Love* in 1986.[8] I took another look at *Prisoner of Love* and began to wonder whether a reading of Genet's texts solely in relation to the notion of feminine writing would do justice to the depth and complexity of his work. But where to look? Mindful of a slogan pervasive in the French Left of the '60s and '70s, "*Retournez aux sources, camarade!*" [Go back to the sources, comrade!], I revisited that classic work, Sartre's *Saint Genet*.[9] It was immediately clear to me that my study of Genet could not ignore, indeed needed to engage, Sartre particularly in the two areas of the massive study that interested me most and that, almost half a century after its publication, called for reassessment: Sartre's analysis of gender and sexuality in Genet and his claim that Genet would never be capable of political engagement.

To begin talking about the long, complex *Saint Genet* rambling in its repetitions and digressions, it is perhaps best to focus on a passage taken from the end of the book where Sartre recapitulates his project:[10]

I have tried to do the following; to indicate the limit of psychoanalytical interpretation and Marxist explanation and to demonstrate that freedom alone can account for a person in his totality; to show this freedom at grips with destiny, crushed at first by its mischances, then, turning upon them and digesting them little by little; to prove that genius is not a gift but the way out one invents in desperate cases; to learn the choice that a writer makes of himself, of his life and of the meaning of the universe, including even the formal characteristics of his style and composition, even the structure of his images and the particularity of his tastes; to review in detail the history of his liberation. (*SG*, 584)

It is quite clear from this passage that the theoretical backdrop to the *Saint Genet* is the philosophy that Sartre was elaborating at the time and that he outlined a few years later in *Search for a Method*.[11] There, he makes a case for the interaction and mutual refinement of marxism, psychoanalysis and existentialism, with existentialism admittedly the most powerful of the three tools. He argues, for example, that "men make their history on the basis of real, prior conditions, but it is the men who make it, not the conditions" (111). This process, in the case of Genet, is precisely the one mentioned in the previous quote: "the way out one invents in desperate cases . . . the choice that a writer makes of himself" (584).

The connections between Sartre's philosophical work and his work of literary criticism are evident and numerous. Take, for example, what can be viewed as one of the guiding principles of *Search for a Method*: "Man is characterized above all by his going beyond a situation and by what he succeeds in making of what he has been made" (137). A very specific example of this process—of making something of what one has been made—is given as the starting point of *Saint Genet*. Sartre, in great detail, describes what he calls "the original crisis": how the young Jean Genet, living in the hostile environment of a foster home in the Morvan, is constituted by the words, gaze and gestures of those around him as a thief. His response is to actively choose to become, on his own terms, what the others had erroneously made of him.

Saint Genet is structured around Sartre's account of what he takes to be Genet's three metamorphoses, the first among which is the process whereby, as described above, the child transforms himself into a thief and embraces a cult of evil. The second metamorphosis, with which the entire "Book Three" of *Saint Genet* is concerned, is of a thief into an aesthete: ". . . a new sun rises: beauty." This aesthete favors style over content, appearances over reality and celebrates processes of denaturalization. Sartre traces back to this period Genet's statement that "the only criterion of an act is its elegance" and suggests that it echoes Oscar Wilde's claim that "in matters of great importance, the vital element is not sincerity but style" (*SG*, 379). This ideology, which one might in general terms call nonutilitarian, extends to Genet's use of language: "He rarely uses language for communicating—it is therefore not a system of signs, nor a discourse on the world: it is the world with Genet inside" (*SG*, 393). The third and final metamorphosis is of aesthete into writer and involves a change of Genet's linguistic attitude, the dawning of a new intention: the intention to make himself understood. Contrary to the earlier situation where, as an aesthete, Genet used language "to immerse himself in its sweet delights" he now uses language also to communicate. With *Our Lady of the Flowers, A Thief's Journal, Miracle of the Rose, Funeral Rites, Querelle,* and *The Maids,* Genet has reached his end[12]—and has become (in the eyes of Sartre and Cocteau at least, for this is how they put it in their famous 1948 letter to the President of the Republic) "a writer universally admired and respected."[13]

Throughout Sartre's accounts of these three metamorphoses, he dwells at great length on what today one might call the sexual politics (gender constitution and erotic relations) in Genet's work and life.[14] This is a highly problematic area of *Saint Genet* and one should bear in mind that Sartre's writings on heterosexual sex (in his *Roads to Freedom,* for example, or some of the plays) are not quite what comes to mind when one searches for the most memorable passages of his work. It is simply not to the erotic realm that Sartre has dedicated his most sophisticated thinking or subtle writing; nor is it one that he appears to approach with the passion that characterizes his engagement with many other subjects. In general, when Sartre writes about sex, he adopts a tone of clinical neutrality sometimes tinged with hints of either boredom or amusement. Yet in *Saint Genet* (or in the episodes of *Roads to Freedom* that have to do with homosexuality) the tone does not always remain neutral.[15] Often, clear discomfort—to say the very least—with homoeroticism transpires.

Sartre is quite far from theoretical detachment when he writes with words that are loaded with abjection: "But the fairy is only a receptacle, a vase, a spittoon which one uses and thinks no more of and which one discards by the very uses one makes of it" (*SG*, 110). Elsewhere, Sartre has no qualms in resorting to excremental imagery: for example, "the homosexual does not know in the griping ache of his pain, whether he is expelling excrement or opening himself up to another body" (*SG*, 109). There is little doubt that this homophobia contributes to much of the reductionism and inaccuracies in Sartre's analysis. There are other problems, too. One is the simplistic model on which Sartre relies to depict the highly complex and fluctuating sexual relations in Genet: a model that is a replica of the (itself inaccurate) binary structure of heterosexual coupling, entailing two partners, one active and one passive, and one act, penetration, performed unto/into the passive one. Sartre's understanding of such interactions very much echoes the analyses offered by Simone de Beauvoir in *The Second Sex*, which highly stress the masochistic nature of female sexuality, for he over and over comments upon the masochism of the passive homosexual.[16] The parallels between de Beauvoir's model and his are often striking. For example, she notes:

> We have seen that the act of love requires of woman profound abandonment. But when the man moves away from her, she finds herself back on earth, on a bed, in the light; . . . she is one vanquished, prey, object.[17]

In *Saint Genet*, Sartre writes:

> The other has withdrawn from [the girl queen]. She is empty. Nothing remains of the madness that convulsed her, nothing but a bit of pain and blood. To the very end the Other has remained to Other; this pursuit of the impossible will have to be resumed over and over, indefinitely. (*SG*, 113–14)

Furthermore, to the binary opposition of heterosexual coupling, Sartre adds the hierarchy of a homosocial feudal model according to which humanity is divided between what he calls "toughs" and "softs." The "toughs" are defined by their strength and meanness and offer some form of protection to the "softs." In return, they require homage; and unlike the matrimonial model where monogamy is in principle assumed by both sides, the tough has no such demands made on him. Such dynamics, however, which Sartre tends to overgeneralize, appear primarily in the penitentiary world of *Miracle of the Rose* and not so much elsewhere. Without going so far as to say that the erotic vision that Genet offers in his novels of the 1940s entirely prefigures late twentieth century utopias such as those suggested by Dennis Altman or illustrated by Robert Gluck, I would nonetheless argue that it often challenges and ultimately undoes the hierarchies and binary structures through which gender is normally constructed.[18] This was not apparent to Sartre and, in any case, would have been of little interest to him. It is certainly more manifest to the late twentieth century reader: easier to see now and easier to analyze with the tools made available through the prodigious developments, over the last two decades, in the fields of Queer Studies and Gender Studies. Such developments, one might add, while they have rapidly pervaded the American intellectual landscape at large, still remain oddly germane to French academic concerns where Sartre's analysis might at first appear less outdated than I have suggested.

The last and penultimate chapters of *Saint Genet* uncover its second major shortcoming. After tracing Genet's development from birth to the present (1951), Sartre assesses his current and future situation. The problem here is quite different from that of the analysis of the sexual politics: it is not that Sartre relies on an inadequate model but, rather, that he summarily dismisses the possibility of a political content in Genet's future life or work:

> Genet, who is an outcast of a "liberal" society, demands, in the name of liberalism, freedom to live for the monster that he has become. This means that he persists in his failures, that he heightens his exile and since he is now only a nothingness, he becomes a proud consciousness of not being. (*SG*, 640)

Sartre's tone is neither optimistic nor generous: "he becomes a proud consciousness of not being." He further describes Genet's psyche as one that is "in relation with the world only to make the world useless." He remarks that Genet "doesn't give a damn about the suffering of others" and predicts that henceforth he will live in heightened exile, and produce work that will be a "pure verbal symphony which is to give an equivalence of silence." Obviously, Sartre did not foresee the prodigious political activity that was to fill the last two decades of Genet's life, and while he wrote brilliantly about Genet's transformation from thief to aesthete, then from aesthete to writer, he did not predict that—in a splendid reversal—it would be Genet, the poet, who, in 1974, would accuse him, the thinker, of being unwilling to confront anything other than his own ghosts; that Genet, that same year, would publish articles in *L'Humanité*, the militant journal of the French Communist Party; or that Genet who, having once refused to join Sartre in a tour of the Soviet Union ("Sartre asked me to go with him; I think he was afraid of being bored. . . . I was afraid of being bored"[19]), was to live and work with the Black Panthers in the United States and with Palestinians in the Middle East. Several essays in the press of the late '60s and early '70s and *Prisoner of Love*, the posthumously published volume which, in 1986, broke Genet's literary silence of twenty-five years, followed. Few readers, in fact, expected this massive volume, these five hundred meandering pages, this collage of "souvenirs" of the time Genet spent with the Panthers and Palestinians that express his support, practical and theoretical, for their struggle.

Sartre, then, was wrong to view Genet's metamorphosis into a writer as the final one. There was yet another, of which *The Blacks* and *The Screens* might have been literary anticipations and which manifested itself at first as clear political engagement in May 1968 when Genet expressed support for the French student/worker revolt and, later that year, for the U.S. antiwar movement.[20] Genet himself outlines his literary itinerary and identifies the break that occurred during that crucial year in his introductory remarks to a debate organized by the Black Panthers at MIT in 1970:

> The five books that I wrote were written in prison, and you will understand that my solitude at the time forced me to have recourse only to myself and to the carceral world. This was followed by five or six years of silence, then I suddenly wrote five plays, and the last one, *The Screens*, was nothing other than a long meditation on the Algerian War. And that happened twelve years ago. In May '68, I realized that I was entirely and without seeking it on the side of the rebelling students and workers. In May, the France that I have hated so much no longer existed, but rather, during one month, a world suddenly freed from nationalism, a smiling world, of extreme elegance, if you will.* (*ED*, 41)

In a slightly (and uncharacteristically) apologetic manner, Genet here explains that his first works (his novels) did not address the world at large simply because of the prison context in which they were written. Indeed, it was in jail, serving successive short sentences for petty thefts, that Genet spent a period crucial to the formation of the political outlook and values of French intellectuals of his generation: World War II. Behind bars for most of 1940–45, removed from the arena where the drama of the war and the occupation played itself out, his perception of the conflict was quite unique. *Our Lady of the Flowers*, written during that period, tells of the vantage point from which he experienced German planes flying over Paris:

> In the twinkling of an eye, I saw a lone child, borne by his iron bird, laughingly strewing death. For him alone were unleashed the sirens, the bells, the hundred-and-one cannon shots reserved for the Dauphin, the cries of hatred and fear. I saw, as I say, or thought I saw an 18-year-old child in the plane and from the depths of my 426 I smiled at him lovingly. (*OLF,* 52)

One of the reasons for Sartre's misjudgment of Genet's political potential might be that World War II, which had done so much to form his own ethical and political thought, functioned for Genet in an entirely different manner: as a rich source of sexual fantasies that found their literary expression in *Funeral Rites.* Indeed, it might have appeared to Sartre that if Genet had so completely failed to be moved towards a rigorous and efficient antifascist stance during the war, he would never be capable of further righteous engagement. Sartre was wrong.

The Algerian war of independence seems to have produced some kind of awakening in Genet, though not a definitive one, and *The Screens* was closely related to this event. Genet describes it as "nothing other than a long meditation on the Algerian War" (*ED,* 41) and the term "meditation" suggests that while the war was at the source of the text, the play does not necessarily participate in the struggle for colonial independence. It is also important to note that while there is no doubt that Genet was utterly sickened by and absolutely opposed to French colonial presence in Algeria and elsewhere, he did not take public positions on the issue during the Algerian war. He did not even lend his name to the famous "Manifeste des 121," a petition signed by 121 artists and intellectuals calling for immediate French withdrawal, and when *The Screens* was first produced in France, Genet warned the director, Roger Blin, to "not make a political tract out of it."[21] Later, though, in an interview with Bertrand Poirot-Delpech, in 1982, he acknowledged that there might be a more directly oppositional quality to the play, saying that it was "a play against France."[22] According to Genet himself, what was a much more formative event was May '68: "In May '68, I realized that I was entirely and without seeking it on the side of the students" (*ED*, 41). Soon after, in 1970, when members of the Black Panther Party requested Genet's support, his response was immediate and his commitment absolute. Within a few days he was at their side in the United States. That same year, when he heard about the violent events of Black September (which pitted the Jordanian military against Palestinian refugees), he immediately left for Jordan and stayed there, working with and for the Palestinians during a period of eight months. Interestingly, it was a shared political position (their support of the students in May '68) that helped establish a friendship between Genet and the other French philosopher who, almost twenty years after Sartre, produced a significant commentary on his work: Jacques Derrida. Though Genet and Derrida had met earlier through literary circles, their relationship deepened during the revolt, nourished by their shared delight at the temporary destabilization of the French government and, White points out, by their common interest in soccer games.[23] In 1974, Derrida published what might be considered his most curious text, *Glas*, which can be succinctly described as a discourse on Hegel and Genet.[24] There is, however, nothing succinct about *Glas*—and this is one of the few things that it and *Saint Genet* have in common. An immediately striking feature of Derrida's work is the playfulness of the *mise en page:* the commentary on Hegel is on the left-hand section of the page, and the section on Genet on the right-hand side. This is not all, of course: each section sometimes consists of a single column, but more often than not it is itself split in two, either partially or along its entire length. Further, there are numerous variations in typescripts, capitalization and indentation. On occasion, sections of text are without warning embedded within others, a *mise en abime* that can involve as little as a few words or as much as several pages. The actual content of the text is as fragmented as its layout. The Genet "section" of *Glas* (or, as Derrida put it, "session"[25]) not only consists of passages from Genet's work and of Derrida's reflections thereon, but also includes references to or quotations from a multitude of sources (from Lacan, Saussure, Pliny, Mallarmé, Poe, to name a few), quotations that are not always presented as such, making it often unclear where they start or end. Similar work is performed in the Hegel section and, through this approach, as well as by juxtaposing two seemingly unrelated authors (and by eschewing what might be regarded as a traditional comparatist approach), Derrida erodes the idea of a book conceived as a self-enclosed system, a finite totality held within the confines of an author's sovereign presence.

What Derrida performs in this text is a scintillating unpacking of associations. *Glas* is traversed throughout by forces of dissemination as it scatters in a multitude of directions and then, in a contradictory centripetal movement, brings back to its core myriad other facets of knowledge and texts. Here, as in much of Derrida's work, there is an absence of methodological constraints. While obviously it is founded on the recognition of the stratified nature of texts and exhibits the general deconstructive moves of dismantling conceptual oppositions and taking apart hierarchical systems of thought, it stands in glaring opposition to *Saint Genet*'s structured approach. What is truly remarkable and a testimony, no doubt, to its infinite richness and complexity is the extent to which Genet's texts lend themselves admirably (though not totally) to radically different approaches, to the bind of Sartre's logocentric will as well as to the turmoil of Derrida's disseminating force. Derrida's fluid, unbound approach, with all of its explosive touches and maddening instablity, with its avoidance of interpretive approaches and disregard for conceptual clarity, in many ways covers more ground than Sartre's and reaches deeper within the substance of the text. And, by its very nature, it avoids *Saint Genet*'s serious shortcomings. Yet (or, rather, hence) it is difficult to work from or with *Glas*, unless, of course, one is a Derridean, and by now it must be amply clear that I am not. Further, because Derrida's response was written prior to Genet's essays of the 1970s and *Prisoner of Love*, it does not touch upon the question of the political in his work. This is not, however, to minimize its importance. Though not an active participant in this study, *Glas* will remain a significant backdrop, a vital reminder of primacy of textuality and *écriture* in general, as well as a testimony to the particular rhetorical complexity and playfulness of Genet's.

> The truth is that Genet's undertaking constantly shifts
> from essentialism to existentialism.
> —J.-P. Sartre

I have up to now dwelled upon those areas of *Saint Genet* that call for further analysis. This does not mean, however, that the relationship of my work to Sartre's will solely be one of revision. On the contrary, this study will be centered around one of Sartre's most powerful and admirable insights, an insight that runs as a persistent thread throughout the otherwise rambling and highly digressive tome. I am referring, of course, to what I quoted above, to Sartre's recognition of the co-presence of existentialism and essentialism in Genet's work (*SG*, 120). Sartre further explains this movement of oscillation, this constant shifting and at times fusion of two systems in this way: "Genet thus forcibly couples a pure will which will define him afterwards by the totality of his acts and a substance which is pre-existent to his actions" (*SG*, 60).

What is fascinating here, and highly relevant to contemporary intellectual concerns, is that existentialism and essentialism, which Sartre sees here as dynamically co-existing and engaging each other, are usually thought of as highly incompatible. In the realm of sexual politics, the first system, essentialism, implies a subject constituted by a stable, preexistent identity enclosed within an equally stable body. The emphasis here is on predetermination and substance. On the other hand, existentialism, with its emphasis on actions, will and freedom, entails a subject that constitutes its own self, including its own gendered self. A core example of the co-existence and tension of these two systems, which I discuss further in the book but that is worth citing at the moment, is the following. It is from Genet's last work, *Prisoner of Love:*

> When after long days of doubt and anxiety a youth—transsexual is rather a horrible word—decides on a sex-change, once the decision is made he is filled with joy at the thought of his new sex, of the breasts he'll really stroke with hands too small and damp, of the disappearance of body hair. But above all, as the old sex fades and, he hopes, finally drops off useless, he'll be possessed with a joy close to madness when he refers to himself as "she" instead of "he," and realizes that grammar also has divided into two, and the feminine half has turned a somersault so that it applies to him, whereas the other half used to be forced on him. The transition to the non-hairy half must be both delightful and terrible. . . . He'll start to be frightened

when his feet refuse to get smaller: you won't find any high-heeled shoes in 9 or 10. (*PL*, 52–53)

At first Genet writes of the plasticity of a body that the transsexual has changed at will; then, of the thrill of the "somersault" of language, the malleable naming of the self. At the end, however, intrudes a very material resistance: the size of the feet that neither hormones nor surgery will alter. These feet represent the irreducible substance of essentialism that derails what appeared to be at first a freely adopted and triumphant constitution of a gendered self.

The co-existence of these broad categories, which Sartre terms existentialism (as he understood it in 1952) and essentialism, pervades Genet's representation of the political realm as well, and the modalities of their interaction will very much inform my chapters on the Black Panthers and the Palestinians. In those analyses, I will broaden those categories beyond their strict definition and include on the side of essentialism not only the conventionally accepted notions such as substance, materiality, stability, pre-determination and nature, but also others such as rigid borders, entrenched symbols and fixed class consciousness.[26] On the side of existentialism there will be, of course, concepts such as agency, free will, self-determination, choice, consciousness, but also others such as malleability, movement and openness, style, metamorphosis, spectacle and images. I will talk, for example, about how Genet was drawn to the Panthers' and Palestinians' struggle because of their reliance on such tactics as performance and masquerade and the deployment of images. For example, he delights in describing the Panthers as "this group of people who instead of hiding showed themselves off," detailing their "extravagant but elegant way of dressing," the leather jackets over arrays of satin and velvet, their "multicolored caps only just resting on their springy hair" (*PL*, 213). Refusing to be reduced to a uniform mass of blackness, intent on preventing others from denying their existence, the Panthers made sure that White Americans were now confronted with the sight of them: "From its foundation in October 1966 right up 'til the end of 1970, the Black Panther's Party kept on surpassing itself with streams of almost uninterrupted images" (*PL*, 47). At the same time, though, Genet very much stresses the importance of the Panthers' reliance on more traditional revolutionary strategies that involve the body not stylistically as a site of startling images but as substance in its very material involvement in armed struggle.

In his representation of the Palestinians Genet often stresses how he perceives material goals to be irrelevant to the fedayeen. He writes of their lack of interest in a simple recovery of territories and the traditional appendages of nationhood:

> The idea of accepting some territory, however small, where the Palestinians would have a government, a capital, mosques, churches, cemeteries, town halls, war memorials, racecourses, and airfields where soldiers would present arms twice a day to foreign heads of state—the idea was such heresy that even to entertain it as a hypothesis was a mortal sin, a betrayal of the revolution. (*PL*, 266)

Similarly, in a 1970s interview with Hubert Fichte, Genet declares he has no interest in visiting Cuba since it had become a conventional nation, albeit communist, with a flag and a national anthem; clearly it is the dynamic process of revolution, not its outcome, that interests him and (in his opinion) the Palestinians. At the same time, he recognizes the hardships of landlessness and the cruel material reality of a displaced refugee population. He warns:

> We oughtn't to have let their ornamental appearance persuade us that the tents were happy places. We shouldn't be taken in by the sunny photographs. A gust of wind blew the canvas, the zinc and the corrugated iron away, and I saw the misery plain. (*PL*, 12)

Here, then, he denounces an illusion, drawing on and sustaining an inside/outside, appearance/reality opposition that he usually undoes. The core of pain beneath the shell is uncovered and this moment of unveiling is not unlike another in *Our Lady of the Flowers* where drag queens at a trial are called by their official names:

> Thus, in the eyes of our bewildered Lady, the little faggots from Pigalle to Place Blanche lost their loveliest adornment, their names lost their corolla, like the paper flowers that the dancer holds at his fingertips and which, when the ballet is over, is a mere wire stem. They were no longer the groove of crinkly paper that flowered on the terrace of cafés. They were misery in motley. (*OLF*, 281)

In *Queens and Revolutionaries*, then, I propose new readings of Genet that focus on two areas, sex and politics, to which *Saint Genet* does not do justice. At the same time, these readings are very much indebted to Sartre, for they are informed by and further explore the oscillation between essentialism and existentialism that he so brilliantly describes.

In the first chapter, "To Sculpt a Stone," I begin by discussing the role of agency in the subject's elaboration of an identity. Concentrating on Divine and other drag queens, I examine its function in the metamorphosis from masculine to feminine, from passive to active, from reactive to performative. Though drag is most often shown to be a triumphant practice, Genet is not without including painful failures of agency. He acknowledges that there are certain aspects of the material world that the subject's will cannot overcome and occasions when shame can be neither concealed nor transcended. I then turn my attention to the manifestations and functions of camp in the construction of gender (an element of Genet's work that escaped Sartre) and show that while it embraces processes of stylization of the body it also recognizes what one might term its base materiality. Also discussed is camp's production of abundance and excess and its transformation of the serious into the frivolous. Finally, I inquire into how Genet's drag fruitfully engages feminist debates on the subject and how it negotiates a middle ground between those that celebrate cross-dressing as a liberating practice and those that view it as politically unsound.

In the second chapter, "The Flower of Their Strength," I show that erotic relations do not conform to the simple bipolar active/passive model that Sartre applies but, on many occasions, allow for reversals, fluctuations and instability. These disruptions of heterosexual norms occur not only in sexual behaviors but in social ones as well, when, for example, Divine and Darling both enact and undermine conjugal conventions. I also address here Genet's representation of masculine bodies and show how their muscular materiality is not always immutable for it sometimes effaces itself into a haze, a halo, a blurring of contours. Similarly, the phallus does not always operate according to Sartre's description of a rigid instrument. Erections are often described in feminine terms (a flowering, a blooming) and, at their most erotic, appear not as naked flesh but as an outline under cloth—which brings me to a discussion of the motif of the veiled phallus.

The third chapter, "The Shadow of a Gun," addresses Genet's writing on the Black Panthers as they appear principally in a number of essays collected in the as yet untranslated volume *L'Ennemi déclaré*. I first return to Genet's perception of events such as the Algerian war, the French student rebellion and the Chicago Democratic Convention of 1968, events that catalyzed his political awakening and through which he began to lend revolutionary efficacy to the realm of representation as well as to actions of a tangible order. Drawing on speeches, press articles and passages from *Prisoner of Love*, I then address what Genet views as the Panthers' self-representation and which, with its highly theatrical elements in clothing, carriage, speech and action, was very pleasing to him. What he calls their metamorphosis from invisible to visible was in large part propagated by the media, and I discuss Genet's ambivalent feelings about this process. I then show that what he views as the poetics of this metamorphosis very much correlates with poetic ideals expressed in his early novels. Finally, turning to some later articles and to George Jackson's *Soledad Brother*, I examine his very unconventional understanding of the role of literature in revolutionary struggle (at the center of which is the tension between informative and poetic language), a role that is on the order of Greek epics or medieval *chansons* and far removed from that of documentary accounts.[27]

The final chapter, "Bullets at the Milky Way," addresses principally Genet's posthumously published *Prisoner of Love*, the account of fragmented recollections of time spent in various Palestinian refugee camps and military bases. I begin by talking about the attraction that North Africa and the Middle East long held for Genet and about his understanding of this particular political commitment. I explore some of the paradoxes created by two simultaneous facts: that while Genet is aware of the cruel and dehumanizing consequences of landlessness, he is also repelled by any form of nationalism; and while he recognizes the oppressive nature of uprootedness when enforced by the outside, he celebrates it when it is freely chosen. I examine the motif of dispersal which pervades *Prisoner of Love* (as in, for example, his depiction of fedayeen as nomadic warriors, the network of tracks in the desert that indicate the reverberation of the Palestinian struggle throughout the Arab world or the decentralized tactics of guerrilla warfare and terrorism) and suggest how this motif contributes to a revolutionary mode that enchants Genet. He also delights in the celebratory atmosphere that pervades the bases as well as in the reliance on performance and imposture on which both Israelis and Palestinians depend. I show that at the same time, however, Genet very much cautions about an overreliance on performance that is not sustained by tangible military actions and implies that there is a certain type of removal from reality that runs counter to political efficacy.

1

To Sculpt a Stone

> To sculpt a stone in the shape of a stone is to remain silent.
> —"Fragments"

THE TRIUMPHS OF AGENCY

DIVINE, THE DRAG QUEEN IN *Our Lady of the Flowers*, IS NOT WITHOUT physical strength. But "a modesty makes her shy away from the facial and bodily grimaces that effort requires" (*OLF*, 90). Reactive rather than performative, such involuntary grimaces would be expressions of the raw body. They would be unseductive signs on and of the body-as-matter: the body in effort becomes simply matter struggling against matter, muscles tightening, contracting under the pressure of an opposing force, with repercussions on the face which is no longer poised, no longer composed. In *The Thief's Journal*, a group of drag queens, known as the Carolinas, parade in a solemn procession to lay a bouquet of roses on the site of a destroyed urinal. The narrator identifies with the group: "I knew that my place was in their midst, not because I was one of them, but because their shrill voices, their cries, their extravagant gestures seemed to me to have no other aim than to try to pierce the shell of the world's contempt" (*TJ*, 65). The attempt here is to transcend ridicule and deflate contempt with an excessive production of precisely what brings on ridicule in the first place. What both these examples have in common is an absolute refusal to show signs of passivity, to be submitted to something outside one's own agency. Divine would rather not use her physical strength than let show, on her face, involuntary reactions to physical strain. And, rather than be submitted to scorn, the queens seek to

draw excessive scorn.[1] The central role of agency in the subject's
elaboration of an identity and a sexuality, and in bringing about a
metamorphosis not only from masculine to feminine, but also from
passive to active and from reactive to performative, is what will be discussed here.

The Carolinas' strategy, whereby a passive recipient of scorn turns
agent to elicit even more scorn, can be viewed as a particular instance
of what Genet, in *The Thief's Journal*, on several occasions describes as
the rehabilitation of the ignoble. This strategy runs throughout the
novel: "Entering further into abjection, pride will be stronger (if the
beggar is myself), when I have the knowledge—strength or weakness—to take advantage of such a fate" (*TJ*, 27). The fall into deeper
abjection is considered to be the outcome of a choice (as when the
narrator, with echoes of catholic self-abnegation forces himself to
love the ugliest and weakest of beggars) or of an attitude whereby an
unfortunate situation is *viewed* as the outcome of a choice (even
though it is not, as when the narrator says he *forced* himself "to consider that wretched life as a deliberate necessity" (*TJ*, 19).[2] The process of transformation of the ignoble is often tied to that of literary
representation. When Genet speaks of his victory—"My victory is verbal and I owe it to the richness of the terms" (*TJ*, 59)—it is to a stylistic process that he refers: "I want to rehabilitate this period by writing
of it with names of things most noble," with words "charged in my
mind with more glamour than meaning" (*TJ*, 58–59). The poetic
treatment, at times, is only a filmy coating: "I wanted to call [the con-
victs] by charming names, to designate their crimes with, for modesty's sake, the subtlest metaphor (beneath which veil I would not
have been unaware of the murderer's rich muscularity, of the violence of his sexual organ)" (*TJ*, 10). Elsewhere, it engulfs its object,
produces a complete metamorphosis: "Should I have to portray a
convict—or a criminal—I shall so bedeck him with flowers that, as he
disappears beneath them, he will himself become a flower, a gigantic
and new one" (*TJ*, 9). And so it is with gender, which is always denat-
uralized, whether by a subtle, surface modification or by a complete
transformation. To not operate that metamorphosis would be to fail
at artistic creation—indeed, at any form of expression: "to sculpt a
stone in the shape of a stone is to remain silent."*[3]

When Genet writes that "Culafroy became Divine" (*OLF*, 283) he
suggests a metamorphosis on the same order as the convict who becomes a flower, "a gigantic and new one."[4] This is the type of drag

with which this chapter concerns itself. When Divine creates a gendered self different from the one that one would conventionally expect a boy to become, the movement is not one of fluctuation (such as those I have described in the previous chapter) but tends towards a more definite point: the attainment of a feminine identity.[5] The transformation warrants a new name, a drag name, chosen by others, and which, phonetically and/or semantically, will be highly feminine: L'Abesse, La Baronne, Reine de Roumanie, Mimosa II, Reine Oriane.[6] The new identity is also recognized grammatically, for Genet invariably refers to Divine in the feminine and uses the masculine only when he is talking of the boy that Divine once was, Louis Culafroy. Even when, at Our Lady's trial, the queens called forth to witness are divested of their drag attire and names, and hence reduced, Genet says, to carcasses, he still refers to them in the feminine. Pomme d'Api has reverted to Eugène Marceau, Première Communion to Antoine Berthollet and Mimosa II to René Hirsch—but all remain "elle." If, however, the public's—and the narrator's—recognition of the drag queen's femininity is important, it is not that which produces the transformation. Rather, the role of the subject's agency in the elaboration of a new identity is crucial.

Divine's self-production is not an easy one. The material on which she works is difficult: "The sitting posture of Michelangelo's Moses is said to have been necessitated by the compact form of a block of marble he had to work with. Divine is always presented with odd-shaped marbles that make her achieve masterpieces" (*OLF*, 198–99). An early experience of this production befalls the young Louis Culafroy:

> He had been strolling through the lanes; when he reached the end of one of them, he saw that he would have to turn around so as not to walk on the lawn. As he watched himself moving, he thought: "he spun about," and the word "spun," immediately caught on the wing, made him about-face smartly. He was about to begin a dance with restrained, barely indicated gesticulations, everything to be merely suggested, but the sole of his yawning shoe dragged over the sand and made a shamefully vulgar sound (for this also should be noted: that Culafroy or Divine, they of the delicate, that is, finical, in short, civil tastes—for in imagination our heroes are attacked, as girls are, by monsters—have always found themselves in situations that repel them). He heard the sound of the sole. This reminder made him lower his head. He assumed with utter naturalness a meditative pos-

ture and sauntered back slowly. The strollers in the park watched
him go by. Culafroy saw that they noticed his paleness, his thinness,
his lowered eyelids, which were as round and heavy as marbles. He
bowed his head more deeply, his grace grew even slower, so much
that all of him was the very image of vocative fervor and that he—not
thought—but whispered aloud a cry:
    "Lord, I am among Thy Elect."
    For a few steps, God carried him off towards His throne. (*OLF*,
199)

The boy perceives the dead end of the alley as an interfering—indeed, an oppositional—circumstance of the material world. To simply turn away would be to submit to contingency and matter. It would
be an act too plainly reactive, as is a grimace too plainly a sign of
physical effort. A verbal representation of himself to himself meta-
morphosizes the banal reaction: "As he watched himself moving, he
thought: 'He spun about.'" ("He spun about" is the not quite ade-
quate translation of "il virevolta." "He twirled" might be better, for
the term suggests grace, dance. The French also contains the famous
"vol," signifying both flight and theft.) To rescue himself from a po-
tentially humiliating situation, Louis would have gone on to further
perform the dance that the twirl introduced, but a second circumstance intervenes: "the shameful vulgarity" of the noise made by his
gaping shoe sole—no doubt vulgar because it recalls base bodily
functions. So as not to be taken aback by this second intrusion of materiality, Louis transforms the initial and aborted performance into
another highly theatrical stance: a priestly walk. It is because of these
interferences—because the marble is oddly shaped—that the result
is a masterpiece: "For a few steps, God carried him off towards his
throne." A classical (seventeenth century) aesthetic is at work: the
harsher the restrictions, the higher the creative tensions, the more
perfect and highly charged the result. In a general manner, it is on a
very recalcitrant material—a body initially inscribed as male—that
Divine performs her chosen self, a feminine self.
    A similar episode occurs when Divine, in a crowded drag queen
bar, wears on her head a little coronet of false pearls. It falls to the
ground and breaks—an intrusion of reality, of the material world, as
was the discovery of the dead end of the alley or the sound of the
shoe. And again, as Sartre puts it, Divine "makes of this downfall an
adornment" (*SG*, 384):

> The crown of pearls falls to the floor and breaks. Condolences, to
> which malicious joy gives rich tonalities: "The Divine is uncrowned!
> . . . She's the great fallen one! . . . The poor Exile!" . . . Then, Divine
> lets out a burst of strident laughter. Everyone pricks up his ears: it's
> her signal. She tears her bridge out of her mouth, puts it on her
> skull, and with her heart in her throat but victorious, she cries out in
> a changed voice: "Dammit all, Ladies, I'll be queen anyhow!" (*OLF*,
> 193–94)

Wrapped in a boa and with a regal air about her, sitting opposite the
highly regarded Darling, Divine embodies poise and dignity—which
crash and shatter with the pearls. The only way not to appear affected
by this sudden loss of dignity (and by the delight of the crowd) is to
show that she has no stake in dignity whatsoever, that, in fact, she is
quite at ease in the grotesque, indeed, that she seeks it. And what
could be more grotesque than the displacement of one bodily part
onto another—a fake part for that matter, one that calls attention to
the decrepit body. Furthermore, with this gesture agency is restored,
and the crowd's attention is drawn away from the accidental.

Divine is mocked by a group of young boys: "They said that pricks
must hurt . . . that old men . . . that women had more charm . . . that
they themselves were pimps" (*OLF*, 200). Upset by the base comments, Divine affects unconcern; she concentrates on drawing pic-
tures on her nails. Then, the transformation occurs. Divine drops the
silently protective, passive attitude and actively engages the young
boys:

> Divine's cheeks are burning. She pretends to be seriously occupied
> with the drawings on her nails and occupied with that only. "Here's
> what I might say," she thought, "to make them think I'm not upset.
> And holding out her hands to the children, with the nails up, she
> smiles and says:
>
> "I'm going to start a fashion. Yes, yes, a new fashion. You see, it's
> pretty. The we-women and the they-women will have lace drawn on
> their hands. We'll send for artists from Persia. They'll paint minia-
> tures that you'll have to look at with a magnifying glass! Oh God!"
>
> The three hoodlums felt foolish, and one of them, speaking for
> the others as well, said:
>
> "Jesus, she's the limit."
>
> They left.
>
> The fashion of decorating fingernails with Persian miniatures
> dates from this episode. (*OLF*, 200)

As well as illustrating the restoration of agency, this passage includes one of the rare occasions when the biological women, referred to as the "they-women," are not spoken of in derogatory terms. Elsewhere we are told, for example, that "no doubt she herself was not a woman (that is, a female in a skirt)" (*OLF*, 225) or that "Divine would have been mortified at seeing herself mistaken for those horrible, titty females" (*OLF*, 230). Unlike the English usage of "female," the French "femelle," in the above sentences, suggests animality. Clearly, the derogatory term refers to a category of women whose gender identity unproblematically derives from sex; also significant is the fact that the female with which Divine does not want to be confused is wearing a simple skirt, unlike Divine who, that evening, is in a black dress embroidered with jet, a pink jacket and a spangled tulle fan. When Our Lady on one occasion wears a dress, and with great panache, he is compared to "the very great ladies of the court," to the courtesans Emilienne D'Alençon and Eugénie Buffet, whose clothes, one imagines, are more spectacular than utilitarian (*OLF*, 221–22). Such comparisons are unquestionably meant to be complimentary. What the "they-women" and "we-women" have in common in the episode of the painted nails is that they both perform a denaturalization.

The following passage is the novel's first description of Divine:

> Divine appeared in Paris to lead her public life about twenty years before her death. She was then thin and vivacious and will remain so until the end of her life, though growing angular. At about two a.m. she entered Graff's Café in Montmartre. The customers were a muddy, still shapeless clay. Divine was limpid water. In the big café with the closed windows drawn on their hollow rods, overcrowded and foundering in smoke, she wafted the coolness of a morning breeze, the astonishing sweetness of the sound of sandals on the stone of the temple, and just as the wind turns leaves, so she turned heads, heads which all at once became light (giddy heads), heads of bankers, shopkeepers, gigolos for ladies, waiters, managers, colonels, scarecrows. (*OLF*, 71)

Divine, as she enters the café for the first time, both embodies scandal (the double scandal, in fact, of prostitution and drag) and creates scandal, described here as a coolness that ripples through the stuffiness of correct bourgeois behavior, revealing its hypocrisy and bringing to the surface the contradiction between what their mouths (spiteful) and eyes (desirous) are saying.[7] Throughout this scene she remains composed, deliberate in her gestures, such as the manner in which she drinks her tea "in tiny sips (a pigeon), putting down and lifting up her cup, with her pinkie in the air" or pats "her snowy forehead with a flowered handkerchief," or the precise manner in which she takes a few coins from her purse and places them noiselessly on the marble table (*OLF*, 73). Again, her gestures, tending towards the refined, are consciously, carefully elaborated and performed. This has been the case, always, since her childhood, when she was Louis: "His every act was served by gestures necessitated not by the act itself but by a choreography that transformed his life into a perpetual ballet" (*OLF*, 163).

As well as illustrating Divine's self-control and the choreographed nature of her behavior, this passage brings up the question of agency in the sexuality of Genet's drag queens.[8] The customers desire Divine. Her seduction, Genet tells us, is implacable. Heads turn towards her as she walks in. They stare at her. Their gaze is fixed, until she looks back and—triumphant—smiles: "She smiled all around, and each one answered only by turning away, but that was a way of answering" (*OLF*, 73). Judith Butler, in *Gender Trouble*, comments on this precise reversal of agency: "For that masculine subject of desire trouble became a scandal, with the sudden intrusion, the unanticipated agency of a female 'object' who inexplicably returns the glance, reverses the gaze, and contests the place and authority of the masculine position."[9]

THE FAILURES OF AGENCY

When Divine returns the gaze at Graff's, a passive object of desire becomes an actively seducing subject. This reversal, however, is threatening to the customers who, rather than succumb, look the other way and agency backfires, for Divine fails to find a client that night. Self-production and self-mastery do not always triumph. There are reverse sides to Genet's celebration of a sovereign subject and free agent. Divine's reluctance to indulge in physical effort can easily be regarded, from the outside, as weakness rather than aesthetic choice, and the onlookers will probably not consider the Carolinas' production of excess as a triumph over scorn. There are other more straightforward, painful, tragic failures which the following pages will address.

In many instances, agency, as it has been traced in the preceding pages, is that which, in the individual, counteracts the manifestations of the physical body or material world. In the same manner that she chooses to evade the grunts and groans expressive of a raw physicality, Divine, in realizing her gender identity, obfuscates a body suggestive of masculinity. However, as mentioned in the "Introduction," Genet writes about the disappointment, caused by a partial resistance to metamorphosis, that mitigates an otherwise triumphant sense of power and delight:

> When after long days of doubt and anxiety a youth—transsexual is rather a horrible word—decides on a sex change, once the decision is made he is filled with joy at the thought of his new sex, of the breasts he'll really stroke with hands too small and damp, of the disappearance of body hair. But above all, as the old sex fades and, he hopes, finally drops off useless, he'll be possessed with a joy close to madness when he refers to himself as "she" instead of "he," and realizes that grammar also has divided into two, and the feminine half has turned into a somersault so that it applies to him, whereas the other half used to be forced on him. The transition to the non-hairy half must be both delightful and terrible. . . . He'll start to be frightened when his feet refuse to get smaller: you won't find many high-heeled shoes in 9 or 10. (*PL*, 52–53)

The joyous reaction to the sex change is tinged with some terror. The terror is of vestigial maleness, of that which resists, that which will not succumb to metamorphosis: here, the size of the feet. Genet is not the only one to have noted this. As Oscar Montero puts it in "Lipstick Vogue": "Any man who has ever tried to slip on a pair of fabulous heels has experienced one of the heartbreaks of drag."[10] He mentions Severo Sarduy's *Cobra*, a novel about a drag queen who is perfect except for her big feet.[11] There are some aspects of the material world—what Sartre calls "the ominous appearing of nature" (*SG*, 382)—that the subject's will cannot overcome.

Agency serves not only to counteract, obfuscate or metamorphosize the manifestations of the material world but also to conceal those emotions such as hurt, pain and humiliation that might contradict a desired impression of invulnerability: when, for example, the fall of Divine's crown is met with delight by the other drag queens, when the young boys mock her femininity or when the gaping sole of Louis Culafroy's shoe suddenly impairs the gracefulness of his stance. On other occasions, however, the individual fails to react and transcend the humiliation. In *Thief's Journal*, after he tries drag for the first time during a Spanish carnival, the narrator reveals: "I then realized how hard it is to reach the light by puncturing the abscess of shame" (*TJ*, 67). This realization occurs because, to ensure that the rupture with "your" (the reader's) world is less brutal, under his feminine outfit (complete with mantilla and fan) he retains a piece of "normal" attire—his pants, which are of course concealed by the long dress. In a crowded bar, someone inadvertently steps on the train of the dress, tears it and reveals the "flaw." We have here a double rupture: the physical rupture of the dress and the rupture of a feminine style that the sudden exposure of the pants brings on—pants that, paradoxically, were designed to ensure continuity. But the continuity was meant to remain known only to the narrator. The breach in an external style, then, is brought on (unintentionally) by the public revelation of an (intentional) internal continuity. As in the episode of Divine's crown, this disclosure causes mocking delight in the crowd. Amidst laughter the narrator is overcome by shame, but he fails to react with Divine's bravado or to airily walk away.

In the episode of the torn dress, the narrator does not even try to command a brilliant and triumphant performance through which agency is recovered. Elsewhere, Genet recounts failed attempts at recovery. The inability of a grand gesture to transcend shame is experienced by Louis Culafroy the very first time he plays with artifice. He has fabricated a makeshift violin with cardboard and a broom-handle and practices secretly at night:

> With humiliation he learned by himself how to place his left fingers on the white threads, according to the instructions he found in the attic. Each silent session exhausted him. His frustration haunted him throughout the lesson, and he studied in a state of constant shame. (*OLF*, 140)

Even if, at first, Louis's desire to "play" the instrument is simply that he wants "to make the same pretty gestures as some youngsters in a magazine" (*OLF*, 139) rather than actually produce music, the experience is not rewarding. His movements, to begin with, are hesitant, and his awkwardness makes him blush. The silence, too, is frustrating: this is a case where gestures alone do not suffice to the performance. To attain the desired degree of sovereignty, they would have to be sustained by sound. Also a failure is Louis's attempt to overcome his shame with theatrical excess:

> One evening Culafroy made a broad, extravagant tragedian's gesture. A gesture that went beyond the room, entered into the night, where it continued onto the stars, among the Bears, and even farther; then, like the snake that bites its tail, it returned to the shadow of the room, and into the child who drowned in it. . . . Once again he realized it was all hopeless. (*OLF*, 140)

This gesture, so grand, Culafroy had hoped would be able to sustain itself without music and, through its self-sufficiency, overcome the shame brought on by a sense of lack. It is a far-reaching gesture, continuing on to the stars, but it transcends nothing and returns to haunt the child with a "laceration that sawed his soul apart" (*OLF*, 140). The oppressed might not feel at ease with those gestures that are reserved for the masters, Genet goes on to write. For example, the good wishes that prisoners, lepers and servants whisper to each other on New Year's Day, shifty, humiliated: "They embarrass us, as the unlined dress-jacket must embarrass the apprentice butler who wears it" (*OLF*, 140). Not all inequalities are transcended by appropriative and excessive gestures, not by a long shot.[12]

After having suffered the humiliating incident of the torn dress, when the narrator brings up the Carolina theme again he does so without the earlier idealization. He does not depict their triumphant bravado but writes with pessimism and gloom:

> Covered with ridicule, the Carolinas were sheltered. No laughter could hurt them; the squalor of their rags testified to their abasement. The sun spared this garland which was emitting its own luminosity. They were all dead. What we saw walking down the street were Shades cut off from the world. (*TJ*, 100)

The heavy layer of scorn will never be exceeded, pierced, ripped open. Rather, it will only be made thicker and more defensive: "No laughter could hurt them. The squalor of their rags testified to their abasement." The dividing line between this, covering oneself with "protective" scorn and positing oneself as agent of self-hatred, is thin.

Sartre understands homosexuality in Genet—and, it seems, homosexuality in general—as the outcome of a choice. There are times when Genet himself suggests the same: "Abandoned by my family, I already felt it was very natural to aggravate this condition by a preference for boys, and this preference by theft, and theft by crime or a complacent attitude in regard to crime" (*TJ*, 87). The mechanism at play here, the restoration of some degree of agency, is by now familiar. Elsewhere, Genet talks about homosexuality in very different terms. In "Fragments," for example, he views it as a fate, almost a malediction: "The sentence that is passed on thieves and assassins is remissible, not ours"*(*F*, 81). Because no tradition teaches the homosexual a set of moral conventions derived from homosexuality itself, his homosexual "nature" (Genet's term) is a source of guilt. It is also a source of self-hatred: "this nature . . . isolates me, cuts me off from both the rest of the world and from other pederasts. We hate ourselves, each of us, and each other"* (*F*, 77). (In this text, Genet uses the terms "homosexualité" and "pédérastie" interchangeably.) The ideas put forth in this text, and its tone, are such that Edmund White claims, in the introduction to the book in which Genet's essay is now published, that "the most religious of zealots could not have denounced the 'hell' of homosexuality with more vigor."[13] Looking back at his own case, Genet goes so far as to now view as bad faith the belief that his refusal of the world was voluntary:

> Attracted to this traditional system that condemned me and from which I had arrogantly excluded myself, my attitude was false and painful (inside of this living organism my pride did not magnificently isolate me so that I became either the first or alone: *it is the organism that exiled me. Pride transformed an exile into a voluntary refusal.* (*F*, 85–86, my emphasis)

These instances of failures of agency, and this last quote which seriously contradicts a project of self-creation ("it is the organism that exiled me"), can be brought to bear on feminist debates of the late twentieth century. "I can be her slave, her servant, her teacher, her mother. . . . I can be anything, anyone," writes Barbara Rose in a collection of essays in defense of lesbian sadomasochism.[14] Divine, one recalls, sculpts herself out of a block of marble. "I become porno-

graphic, a slut, a whore—an identity that was denied me with as
much ferocity as the pleasures of masculinity" writes Pat Califia in
her important article on gender-bending.[15] Divine, more subtly, not
only sustains the stares of the men at Graff's but smiles and returns
their gaze. For many, the recovery of agency in the acting out of gender roles or sexual roles is a feminist project.[16] Sue Ellen Case writes:
"From a theatrical point of view, the butch/femme roles take on the
quality of something more like a character construction and have a
more active quality than what Rivière calls a reaction-formation.[17]
Thus, they lend agency and self-determination to the historically passive subject."[18] It is clear that Genet represents agency as central to
the constitution of a sexual and gendered self, particularly as it counteracts what Sartre calls "the ominous appearing of nature." He
makes an even greater contribution to the debate, one might argue,
when he cautions us against an overly optimistic faith in the power of
agency.

Indeed, there are times when proponents of gender-bending and
sadomasochism rely on overly simple, and overly idealized, notions
of choice, consent and self-determination. It is with these simplifica-
tions that the most valid critiques (that is, those that engage the
question on intellectual rather than moral grounds) of sadomasochism quarrel with the fact that the notions of choice, consent
and self-determination are viewed as autonomous rather than context bound and as affected by histories, both collective and personal,
and by the network of various power relations in which individuals
are already caught. When, in *Coming to Power*, Barbara Rose claims "I
can be anything," the "I" is all-powerful, posited as momentarily dis-
entangled from the cultural, sociopolitical field. It is an "I" that
claims some kind of a dissociation from culture and discourse. Genet
warns us against such claims. At the same time that he cultivates a
simple, early existentialist position that celebrates the victory of
choice and free will over circumstance and matter, he allows for, and
illustrates, its limitations. For, as with the tensions he creates and negotiates between a triumphant and victimized view of homosexuality,
he is not without recognizing the power of public opinion (the scorn
directed at the Carolinas, the mockery made of the torn dress, the
enforced exile of the homosexual) and of the materiality of bodies.
These are obstacles to free will and self-determination that, in certain instances, can be overcome or circumvented (the grunts and
groans that accompany physical effort) while in other cases not (the

size of the feet). The interplay of agency and determinism in the construction of gender is an area where Genet's work is relevant to feminist thought and to the recognition of a subject who is both entangled in her social and physical condition and who, at the same time, has the potential to create change, who is capable of agency and transformation.

Finally, one might wonder whether, to operate in a politically efficient manner, agency and choice have to be recognized as such by others—including others outside of the oppressed group. This point raises issues that are particularly relevant to butch/femme personas. As mentioned earlier, Divine, when she avoids physical effort so as not to show its signs, might appear merely weak, and the Carolinas, with their heightened theatrics, might simply seem out of control. This lack of acknowledgment of the subject's agency and choice obviously weakens the power of such strategies and, also, obliterates an important aspect of gender-bending: that the chosen roles not be designed to reflect a "true nature," that a butch persona, for instance, not be construed as the expression of a masculine "true self."[19] An important question is: how does one signal to the world that such roles are not imposed but consciously chosen and played out? How does one signal that the intentions behind a certain choice of gender or sexual style, and its political signification, are different from what they are conventionally assumed to be? Wendy Chapkis reflects on this in *Beauty Secrets:* "It's Saturday night and I'm on the prowl, decked out in my most provocative clothing. I'm on my way to the local women's bar—a haven of safety in the city. But before I get there, I have to pass through the dark streets where sexually provocative means asking to be attacked. It's hard to assume a 'don't fuck with me' walk in high heels."[20] Case engages the question and suggests that, unlike in the 1950s when such roles were adopted in a manner far more earnest than today, "butch/femme should inhabit the camp space of irony and distance."[21] This, of course, will not always settle the concern raised above regarding the misreading, by straight men, of a sexually provocative dress, for the recognition of irony often demands a reading far more subtle than those men would ever be likely to generate. Still, it is interesting that a gay male sensibility might prove useful to questions of feminist agency. Camp in Genet's drag (which was completely invisible to Sartre)—how it manifests itself, how it functions, what it means—is worth looking into.[22]

CAMP

In a particularly interesting passage of *Saint Genet*, Sartre ponders the notion of luxury and makes a distinction between that which existed in pre-industrial times and the present. Luxury that existed in pre-industrial times and was enjoyed by the aristocracy was the luxury of rare, natural objects—a pearl, gems, fur—freshly torn from their organic or mineral state, still bearing that "taste": "One is a man of taste if one is able, beneath the ostentatious appearance, to discern the carnal, clinging, organic, milky taste of the creature" (*SG*, 361). With the industrial age appears another type of luxury that honors production rather than raw materials. Its object, no longer ripped from nature, is a synthetic imitation. It shows the mark of human labor in "a polish, a softness, a roundness, a sharpness of color that cannot be found in nature. . . . A synthetic pearl reminds us any moment, by its sheen, that man, who only yesterday was a natural creature, can produce in himself and outside of himself a false nature more sparkling and more rigorous than the true one" (*SG*, 361–62). When she is rich for a spell, Divine is not interested in accumulating wealth, material possessions. What she seeks are the gestures of luxury, gestures that are performed amidst things of luxury—not the things themselves: what Sartre calls "a false nature more rigorous and more sparkling than the first one" (*SG*, 362). She does make one concession to pre-industrial luxury. The acquisition of a set of musk-saturated leather luggage which merely serves as a prop as she practices these gestures: seven or eight times a day Divine enters the Pullman car of a train, has her luggage stacked, then has it unstacked only minutes before the train is due to depart, hails a cab and checks into a luxurious hotel. Now she knows "how to walk on carpets and talk to flunkeys" (*OLF*, 100). She has learned to move amidst luxury; she has acquired a new style. And, even more than gestures among luxurious accoutrements, it is form in motion (the feel of the curve of the road) and pure form (the arabesque of wrought iron) that place Divine securely in the position of one-who-is-in-luxury: "But it is particularly when her hired car passes a wrought-iron gate or makes a delicious swerve that she is an infanta" (*OLF*, 100).

The above account of Divine-in-luxury perfectly illustrates an understanding of camp that Esther Newton proposes in a study of drag queen performers:[23] camp suffused with the perception of "life-as-theater" and "being-as-playing-a-role"; to the detriment of content, it focuses absolutely upon style, privileges it above all, and correlates with much of what I discussed in the first section of this chapter. The importance, Newton notes, "shifts from what a thing *is* to how it *looks,* from what is done to how it is done"(my emphasis).[24] Divine-in-luxury also highlights precisely what Susan Sontag, in her "Notes on Camp," views as quintessential of that sensibility: the extravagant gesture (having the luggage stacked and unstacked over and over again) and the curved line (the wrought-iron gate, the swerve of the car).[25] In fact, one of Divine's "signature gestures" follows a curve: "When she took an handkerchief from a pocket, it described an enormous arc before she put it to her lips" (*OLF,* 112). Divine, Genet tells us, is characterized by her gestures, of which there are many. They function in a manner that Judith Butler describes in her essay on Lana Turner's performance in the movie *Imitation of Life:* "Gestures that are not primarily expressive but operate performatively to constitute femininity as a frozen stylization of the body."[26] Divine's "signature gestures" are gestures through which her character is created. They are not brought on by, or necessarily appropriate to, a situation; they are not expressive of an emotion, of an inner self, but, rather, serve to constitute a self.

Nonetheless, camp in Genet, while it embraces processes of stylization of the body, is not without acknowledging, in an often humorous manner, the reality of what might be termed the "base" material body. When Genet writes that Divine avoids physical effort because of the unbecoming grimaces it produces, he explains this attitude in terms of her *pudeur,* which, in addition to sexual modesty, suggests a delicate sensitivity, a refined disposition. Yet Divine loves vulgarity: "Her perfume is violent and vulgar. From it we can already tell that she is fond of vulgarity" (*OLF,* 74). If one understands by vulgarity the overexposure of flesh, the exhibition of the raw body and of base bodily functions, what is operating here, with the co-existence of *pudeur* and vulgarity, is one of the juxtapositions, such as high and low, cheap and expensive, that are characteristic of camp. However, vulgarity can also lean towards antiphysis, artificiality, the violence of a perfume, the gaudy exaggeration of a color. Vulgarity, then, as well as the underprocessed, is the overprocessed. Vulgarity of body is the overexposure of flesh as well as its overornamentation (good taste is a discreet equilibrium). One remembers how Divine, when she is mocked by a group of young boys ("they said that pricks, etc. . . ."), answers by holding out her hand and saying: "I'm going to start a fashion. Yes, yes, a new fashion. You see, it's pretty. The we-women and the they-women will have lace drawn on their hands. We'll send for artists from Persia. They'll paint miniatures that you'll have to look at with a magnifying glass! Oh! God!" (*OLF*, 200). The boys, suddenly in awe, do not respond: here, Divine silences the vulgarity of the underrefined with the vulgarities of the overrefined. High vulgarity and low vulgarity are also at work to create a comic effect in the following episode:

> She always had with her, up her sleeve, a small fan made of muslin and pale ivory. Whenever she said something that disconcerted her, she would pull the fan from her sleeve with the speed of a magician, unfurl it, and suddenly one would see the fluttering wing in which the lower part of her face was hidden. Divine's fan will beat lightly around her face all her life. She inaugurated it in a poultry shop on the Rue Lepic. Divine had gone down with a sister to buy a chicken. They were in the shop when the butcher's son entered. She looked at him and clucked, called the sister and, putting her index finger into the rump of the trussed chicken that lay on the stall, she cried out: "Oh! look! Beauty of Beauties!" and her fan quickly fluttered to her flushing cheeks. She looked again with moist eyes at the butcher's son. (*OLF*, 101)

The style that a fan signifies (independently of its always quite minor utilitarian function) depends on context: coded elegance, possibly but not necessarily tending towards the coquettish; seduction ritual, where the fan playfully hides and reveals—certainly out of place in a poultry shop. The fluttering gesture accompanies one of low vulgarity as Divine puts her finger in the rump of the chicken. These are simultaneous and contradictory signs, the overly refined and the base, and they contain contradictory gender connotations—the femininity of the fan, the masculinity of the penetration. Contradictory gestures aimed at seduction, as Divine—fully in command of her performance—eyes the butcher's son. When grimacing under physical effort, or being told that "pricks must hurt," she is submitted to base vulgarity. Here she is its agent; it is therefore acceptable, particularly in conjunction with the camp gesture, stylized, of the fan. She performs vulgarity, high and low. In the episode of the fallen crown, the coronet that Divine first wears is made of false pearls, like those that prisoners weave into funeral wreathes, Genet tells us. The denture, with which Divine replaces the pearls when they fall to the ground, is also artifice, but artifice that serves and points to the base body, the aging, failing body, and, specifically, to one of its most blatantly prosaic parts—teeth. Camp's relationship to the body combines two seemingly opposed attitudes: a lucid recognition and awareness—sometimes almost clinical—of the materiality of the "base" body, with an overwhelming embrace of processes of stylization that transform it.

Sontag, in her essay on camp, makes a disputable claim: that camp is apolitical. One might disagree with this and suggest that there are in fact two ways in which camp might be of political consequence. One has to do with the transformation of the serious into the frivolous (and sometimes vice versa) and the other with the production of excess. One example that immediately comes to mind, when one thinks about transformations of the serious into the frivolous, occurs around Divine's death, a subject about which her mother reflects: "What would top it all . . . would be for him to die in a fashionable city, in Cannes or Venice, so that I could make pilgrimages to it" (*OLF*, 65). When Divine does die, her funeral is considerably enlivened by the following episode: "The abbé blessed the grave and handed his sprinkler to Darling, who blushed to feel it so heavy, then to the queens, who turned the whole area into a squealing of petty cries and high giggles" (*OLF*, 70). An inverse example of the transformation of the frivolous into the serious is that of the destroyed urinal, which the queens turn into a place of worship. The Carolinas bestow monumental status upon a less than monumental site, replacing the sexual ritual which used to take place there with a highly respectable one, a solemn procession. Dignified, also, is the gesture of laying red roses, tied with black crepe, *in memoriam*, on the much lamented site.

A quintessential "real-life" example of the transformation of the serious into the frivolous is the explanation of a drag queen who, on 27 June 1969, was present at the Stonewall riots. She says that it was Judy Garland's death, really, that was responsible for making the rebellions happen that night.[27] Invoking the effect of the death of the adulated actress, rather than the conditions of oppression and raging police brutality, this explanation is not dissimilar to Genet's denial of a political or moral factor in his acts: "My adventures, never governed by rebellion or a feeling of injustice, will be merely one long mating, burdened and complicated by a heavy, strange, erotic ceremonial (figurative ceremonies, leading to jail and anticipating it)" (*TJ*, 10).

Contrary to Sontag's suggestion, however, these strategies do not mean that camp is apolitical, on the contrary. Humor and irony in camp are a means of communicating and surviving in an intolerable situation. Newton notes: "Camp humor is a system of laughing at one's position rather than crying."[28] Michael Bronski, in *Culture Clash*, also disagrees with Sontag on this issue and explains: "Because it has been used by gay people as a means of communication and survival, camp is political. And because it contains the possibility of structuring and encouraging limitless imagination—to literally create a new reality—it is not only political, but progressive."[29]

Also bearing political ramifications is another feature of camp: its excess, its extravagance. Newton considers this excess typical of the camp attitude towards the role, an attitude that is dual: on the one hand, it is important to put on a good show, a polished performance; on the other, distance must be indicated by hyperbole. I would add another reading of this excess, for Newton's understanding of it as "distance from the role" relies upon the authentic/inauthentic opposition which she elsewhere succeeds in undermining. Cixous's distinction between "the realm of the proper" and "the realm of the gift" is relevant here.[30] "The realm of the proper" is based on a strict economy governed by principles of exchange, debt and profit and is dependent upon classifications, systems—and, as its name indicates, property and the appropriate. It is a typically masculine realm. Women are not caught up in this restrictive, retentive system and its limitations: theirs is the realm of the gift, which enables them to exercise bounty, generosity, without the need for return.[31] It is a realm that encourages exuberance, abundance, excess—excess, which, Verena Conley notes in *Hélène Cixous: Writing the Feminine*, Cixous understands in a sense derived from Bataille: suggesting "effusion, eros, poetry, drunkenness, laughter," and, again, embracing a pleasure principle.[32] Excess in camp, and often represented in Genet, is an abundance beyond that which is necessary to the terms of a strict economy and within which Divine and other drag queens move with grace and ease.

FEMINIST CRITIQUES

The introduction to this study noted the demeaning manner in which Sartre often writes about homosexuality in general and about what he labels as "passive homosexuals" and "girl queens" in particular. Though he does not always include Divine in his unkind generalities and does spend quite some time addressing the specifics that characterize her with an occasional degree of sympathy, Sartre's analyses of her are far from unconflicted. Repeatedly, he identifies Divine the character with Genet the author and does so in unambiguous and unflattering terms: "Divine is Genet himself, since she enacts the horrible homosexual decline which he feels and the signs of which he tries, with the anguish of an aging woman, to detect in every mirror." While he does recognize, as did my analysis, the vital role of gestures in the constitution of a self, particularly as they transcend shame and humiliation and acknowledge their transformative nature, he has an odd and not altogether positive way of describing the process: "[Divine's] gestures redeem the basest material by consuming it in the fire of the unreal" (*SG*, 380). Elsewhere he explains that gestures are acts that are effectual only in appearance and this appearance/reality dichotomy is one that he clings to throughout—problematically. For example, in his analysis of the episode of the fallen crown he claims that there is a truth to Divine and defines it in the following terms: "The truth of Divine is an old man . . . who sticks his dentures back into his mouth before the ironic eyes of the onlookers" (*SG*, 385). Sartre, then, cannot, in his perception of drag, refrain from retaining the distinction between reality and appearance and locates Divine's "truth" in maleness and old age (which makes his emphasis on identification between Divine and Genet a little odd since Genet was only thirty-two years old when he wrote *Our Lady of the Flowers*). This reading, on the contrary, argues that these texts emphasize not at all the gulf between reality and appearance but the fluctuations, oscillations and reversals that occupy the space between the two, and that if one were to locate the "truth" of Divine, it would reside in the various aspects of her process of self-creation rather than in its results (and even less in an evaluation of the success of the results).

Not only is Genet's representation of drag far more interesting and complex than Sartre suggests, it can also fruitfully engage a number of feminist debates on the subject. For example, the emphasis on the fluctuations, oscillations and reversals of cross-dressing such as those described in Genet is something that Sandra Gilbert and Susan Gubar locate solely in its female-authored representations. In *Sexchanges*, the second volume of *No Man's Land*, they discuss the theatrical representations and dramatic reversals to which gender appearance became subject in the late nineteenth and early twentieth centuries.[33] Reacting against Victorian propriety and encouraged by the increasing diversity and availability of items of clothing, "modernist" women, especially upper class women of letters, followed in the aristocratic footsteps of George Sand.[34] In their already highly dramatized daily lives, they experimented with the politics, aesthetics and erotics of costume. Their professed aim oscillated between and sometimes combined functionality and pleasure. The dress-reform advocate Mary Walker, for example, justified her proposals on practical grounds—hygiene, freedom of movement, and so forth. However, a photograph of her in masculine evening wear shows, as Gilbert puts it, a "strutting appropriation":[35] a visibly pleasurable, rather than solely functional, endeavor. In the highly sophisticated portraits by the photographer Romaine Brooks, the erotic—lesbian—element clearly surfaces, as it does in the cross-dressing episodes in the lives of Radclyffe Hall and Vita Sackville-West.

Such "real-life" trends were accompanied by literary representations. Gilbert and Gubar read *Orlando* and *Nightwood* as powerful defiances of the conflation of gender and biological sex.[36] In *Orlando*, the emphasis is less on bodily changes than on the "insouciant shiftings" of costume: the free choices offered by a vast and varied wardrobe from which to construct selves. As Mary Jacobus puts it in "Reading Woman (Reading)":

> In Woolf's novel, Orlando's transvestism is not simply a travesty which mimics or exaggerates the signs by which gender identity is culturally instituted and maintained; rather, Orlando might be said to dress up at (cross-)dressing, exposing the dilemma ("here, again, we come to a dilemma") or impossible choice of gender.[37]

Nightwood celebrates sexual ambiguity, inversion, and again blurs gender identity through a profusion of costume. *Tender Buttons*, while not addressing transvestism, shows clothing to constitute a sign system, either constraining, when strictly referential, or liberating, when the conventional structures of signification are questioned.[38]

Male authors' treatment of costume and cross-dressing is altogether different, Gilbert and Gubar argue, for ultimately it reasserts, and powerfully so, an ideologically sound link between biological sex and gender role. In D. H. Lawrence's *The Fox*, a lesbian relationship is disrupted by the intervention of a male soldier who seduces one of the women, divests her of her male dress, and kills the other.[39] In Hemingway's *The Garden of Eden*, order is restored by the intervention, again, of a solidly gendered savior: a couple's acting-out of gender-reversal fantasies is brought to an end by a Madonna-like "real" woman whose initial lesbian liaison with the wife is soon replaced by a heterosexual one with the husband.[40] Similarly, in *Ulysses*, Bloom's enforced cross-dressing ultimately reestablishes and reinforces male potency:[41] "Joyce's parodic narrative implies that to become a female or to be like a female is not only figuratively but literally to be degraded, to lose one's place in the pre-ordained hierarchy that patriarchal culture associates with gender."[42] After Bloom casts off his female costume, he becomes infused with a new virility and "will increasingly resemble his paternal creator."[43]

For Gilbert and Gubar, the cross-dressing episode in *Ulysses* conforms to a model that they explain in both sociological and psychoanalytical terms. The sociological analysis draws on the connection that Natalie Davis establishes between ritual cross-dressing and the carnivalesque in medieval and Renaissance Europe: rituals whereby a social and sexual order is temporarily inverted only to be better and more safely reinstated.[44] The psychoanalytical explanation draws on the work of Robert Stoller. Specifically, Gilbert and Gubar borrow his view of the transvestite as "phallic woman" and argue that cross-dressing ultimately reinforces gender hierarchy: it is designed to prove that a cross-dressing male is better than a woman because he is a woman with a penis.[45] Neither of these analyses could apply to Genet's texts: the carnivalesque because they never show drag to subside into a return to a conventional social and sexual order—to a heterosexual patriarchy; and the "phallic woman" model is not appropriate because it views cross-dressing in a heterosexual context, as a mechanism to alleviate castration anxiety.[46] Rather, his texts display oscillations, reversals and uncertainties similar to those that Gilbert and Gubar detect in female-authored representations. Indeed, the drag queen's attainment of femininity does not mean that hers is a completely unified gender identity and does not completely exclude the masculine. An obvious example of this is the already mentioned feet of the transsexual, and there are others. Sometimes, instead of the exuberant, hyperbolic, highly adjectival language of queens, Divine resorts to the men's slang, to what Genet calls "the male tongue." On those occasions, her macho companions disapprovingly refer to her as a "broad acting tough" (*OLF*, 90). Elsewhere, the virility of another drag queen, Mimosa, erupts when she screams in anger and jealousy at Divine: " 'Get the hell out of here, you dirty whore, you cocksucker!' It was the milkman" (*OLF*, 114). A more sustained, though still relatively short-lived, enactment of the masculine occurs when Notre-Dame enters the scene, and Divine becomes smitten by him; after having loved men stronger, more muscular than herself—she feels virilified:

> Now she seeks, for a while, new gestures, a new style, a new attitude, which, because she has not yet grown accustomed to it, she does not perform with the grace and self-assurance of her feminine self: She ran from boy to girl, and the transitions from one to another, because the attitude was a new one, were made stumblingly. (*OLF*, 133)

This, then, is yet another example that shows that Divine's true self cannot be pinned down in one gender or another, nor can it be constituted by fixed and well-defined aspects of both as in the model of the phallic woman: feminine items of clothing on the one hand, "prominently displayed cock and balls," to borrow Marjorie Garber's terminology, on the other.[47] Hers is a fluid identity, always under construction, more often than not "exposing the dilemma or impossible choice of gender," as Jacobus puts it in her analysis of *Orlando.*[48]

There are a number of other feminist critiques of drag that Genet's representation interestingly challenges. The first is that drag harshly parodies and demeans the feminine, resulting in what Marilyn Frye calls "a casual and cynical mockery."[49] This criticism, however, is one that equates hyperbole (excess) with parody (where a model is undermined). In reality, one does not imply the other. Drag, as it appears in Genet, while it indulges in excess, does not point to a model, to an original; with the irony and distance that camp hyperbole brings forth, there is the suggestion of an elsewhere where a truthful and authentic original resides. Camp hyperbole, then, as it is represented in Genet, signals not only the inauthenticity of the drag persona (his queens do not expect to pass as women) but also the inexistence of an essential feminine where a specific style and behavior would be the immanent manifestations of an internal gender core. It is also the case that, with its excessive element, its exuberance and its emphasis on the pleasure principle, Genet's drag renders obsolete a strict, masculine system of exchange. Furthermore, on a nontheoretical level, one should also note that the burlesque (which relies on deformity as well as hyperbole) is completely absent from Genet's drag and very rare, overall, in a homosexual context. It is, however, prevalent when female impersonators address themselves to a straight audience (as in the case of British comedian Danny La Rue, whose shows are considered wholesome family entertainment) and where a carnivalesque parody of women takes place. Drag queens, if they feel no special rapport with the woman next door, do not tinge their adulation of the stars they wish to emulate with cruelty.[50]

Another critique, that drag reinforces a reprehensible style and upholds the oppressive definition of what it is to be a woman, emerges from the wave of feminism of the 1970s that promoted sensible, comfortable clothing with both practical and theoretical aims. It is not surprising that for those who consider that discarding such stereotypes and norms is a feminist project in and of itself, to see them adopted and adulated by gay men can be troubling. However, that critique is already answered by one of the points outlined above. Genet's drag shows that the specific styles and behaviors we associate with femininity are not expressive of an internal gender. For, clearly, the traditional definition relies on a causal relationship between the two: one acts like a woman because one is a woman. To this one might add that, unlike the conventional feminine body onto which an illusion of stability, of "eternal feminine," is enforced, drag unabashedly acknowledges its instability and artificiality. It challenges the contours and unity of the body as it is conventionally naturalized, and therefore clearly subverts, rather than upholds, the oppressive definition. And, finally, since drag, for all the reasons given above, rejects the idea of a feminine domain, the criticism that views drag as a male invasion of a feminine domain, an imperialist gesture, yet another attempt to "outdo" women, becomes absurd: it is not possible for a practice to encroach on something the existence of which it disproves. This fear of "colonization" which has also rendered male-to-female transsexuals unwelcome among feminists, and even more so among lesbian feminists, is also understandable. Yet it is based on ideas of propriety and binary oppositions that Genet's drag effectively overcomes.

Genet's texts can be made to intervene in another debate, one referred to earlier in this chapter and that concerns the role of agency in gender creation; in feminist thought this debate often crystallizes around the topic of gender-bending. The interplay between the tri-

umphs and failures of agency in Genet's drag invalidates not only
Sartre's claim that Divine's true self is an old man but also, at the
other end of the spectrum, Barbara Rose's assertion that "I can be
anything, anyone." Divine shows that it is possible to celebrate an individual's power of metamorphosis while not ignoring the restrictions that circumvent that power. It is clear that in the same way that
Genet views homosexuality as both a choice and a fate, he shows the
failures of agency as well as its triumphs. He also recognizes both the
malleability and resistance of bodies: for, if Genet's drag challenges
processes of conventional naturalizations that establish their unity
and stable contours, it also very much stresses the materiality of bodies (or, at least, of body parts). This duality is perhaps best encapsulated by the camp relationship to the body which combines two
seemingly opposed attitudes: a lucid recognition and awareness—
sometimes almost clinical—of the materiality of the "base" body with
an overwhelming embrace of the processes of stylization that transform it.

Furthermore, it is worth noting that, with its emphasis on fragmentation and lack of interiority, drag in Genet suggests a very postmodern gendered self, such as that, for example, described by Judith
Butler in *Gender Trouble*. As well as developing the idea of a performative gender, Butler doubts the very existence of prediscursive,
presocial bodies and hence questions the category of sex as corporeal, material, passive, precultural ground.[51] She draws on Mary
Douglas to argue that the limits of the body are not constituted by a
material reality, but that social taboos establish and maintain its
falsely naturalized boundaries. Such an imposition of "stable bodily
contours" is necessary to social stability, since the physical body is
synecdochic for the social body and unregulated permeability is
threatening: "The body is a model that can stand for any bounded
system. Its boundaries can represent any boundaries which are
threatened or precarious."[52] These boundaries, Butler adds, are secured by and serve compulsory heterosexuality: "The construction of
stable bodily contours relies upon fixed sites of corporeal permeability and impermeability. Those sexual practices in both homosexual
and heterosexual contexts that open surfaces and orifices to erotic
signification or close down others effectively reinscribe the boundaries of the body along new cultural lines."[53]

It appears that drag in Genet challenges the contours and unity of
the body as it is conventionally naturalized. In his gloomy "Frag-

ments" he says it clearly: "Queens, you are made of pieces."* This lack of coherence and of an organizing principle is yet another of the queen's afflictions:

> But—feathers, petticoats, fluttering eyelashes, fans—it is a mournful but frivolous carnival that encumbers you. Where are they to be found, those rigors that regulate themes, master them, write the poem? Where, finally, are the great tragic themes? Queens, you are made of pieces.* (F, 78)

Genet goes on to explain that because of this fragmentation (and of the postmodern lack of "great tragic themes") the queen must direct all her efforts into establishing internal links between the various "pieces." Rather than extending outwards, in a relationship to the world, her life is governed by a search for internal coherence, for an aesthetic, he argues: her life is an "oeuvre d'art." The first description of Divine, as she sits at Graff's, suggests this fragmentation. Her body is made up of several disconnected "parts," infused with and held together only by the charm that unfurls from her eyes: "Her eyes sing, despite their despair, and their melody moves from her eyes to her teeth, to which she gives life, and from her teeth to all her movements, to her slightest acts, and this charm, which emerges from her eyes, unfurls in wave upon wave down to her bare feet" (OLF, 72).

In "Fragments" Genet goes on to define a moral as "a lucid, voluntary attempt to coordinate and harmonize various elements in an individual for an end that transcends him" (F, 80–81). However, since, like a work of art, the gender constitution of a drag queen is an end in itself, the moral it generates refers only to itself and hence, Genet claims, is an aesthetic: "Queens, our moral was an aesthetic." In Genet's camp, the content (the moral) is the form (the aesthetic) rather than expressed by the form. Along with this—the fact that onto the drag body no ideological coherence is projected from the outside and that the queen hence has to create her own—there are very practical, material ways in which the contours are destabilized: with wigs, false eyelashes, false breasts (what Garber calls "spare parts").

Some queens, while not anticipating a genital sex change, might opt for breasts through implants or hormones; the hormones will make the rest of the contour of the body less angular, too, and might also affect body hair and voice (in fact, the increasing availability of various types of plastic surgery and hormone therapies makes the distinction between drag queens and transsexuals less clear than in the past). The drag body, then, displays varying and unstable degrees of artifice, removability. Some changes are permanent, some are not: legs and chests may be smooth because recently shaved or because of hormone therapy; hair might be long, or a wig. Eyelashes might be tinted and curled, or false. In fact, in *The Thief's Journal*, the narrator claims that he discovers artifice through false eyelashes:

> One of the mariconas was called Pedro. He was pale and thin. His waist was very supple, his step quick. His eyes in particular were splendid, his lashes immense. . . . We started quarreling. I punched him. His eyelashes stuck to my knuckles; they were false. I had just discovered the existence of fakes. (*TJ*, 62–63)

Drag, then, undermines what elsewhere prevails, the illusion of stable bodily contours. One might argue that the "conventional" feminine body, like the drag body, is highly unstable for it, too, relies on artifice, on removable parts; yet an illusion of stability, of unchanging, eternal femininity is enforced upon it. Drag's unabashed acknowledgment of instability and artificiality of the feminine ("Pedro airily admitted to his false lashes, the Carolinas to their wild larks" [*TJ*, 65]) might be viewed as a feminist gesture. To end, one might emphasize again that, beyond these theoretical debates, what predominates in *Our Lady of the Flowers* is the celebration of the magnificent metamorphosis of the village boy Louis Culafroy into the reigning queen of Pigalle. It is that metamorphosis that prevails, that is where strength and power are located, perhaps precisely because the performance is a difficult one. One remembers that the marble out of which Divine carves herself offers a double resistance: the resistance of a dense, unyielding substance (unlike a far less noble medium, the "muddy, still shapeless clay" of which the clients at Graff's were made), and that of its odd shape, like the block out of which Michelangelo carved his Moses. The transsexual, dizzy with delight at his hairless skin and new breasts, cannot escape a remnant of his old self, the unshrinkable feet which, as if they had a will of their own, "refuse" to shrink. Also seemingly with a will of its own is the strained body that grimaces and grunts and which can only be escaped by shunning physical effort. The moments of pathos, of vulnerability, where the style is ruptured, do not diminish its beauty and vitality, and, clearly, they do not in any way serve to uphold the value of authenticity. Rather, they serve as a disruptive and destablizing moment, as does the question at the end of the following passage, taken from the last pages of the novel. At Our Lady's trial, the familiar queens appear as witnesses divested of their drag names:

> Our Lady saw Mimosa II enter. The clerk, however, had called out "René Hirsch." When he called "Antoine Berthollet," First Communion appeared; at "Eugène Marceau," Lady-apple appeared; thus, in the eyes of Our bewildered Lady, the little faggots from Pigalle to Place Blanche lost their loveliest adornment, their names lost their corolla, like the paper flowers that the dancer holds at his finger tips and which, when the ballet is over, is a mere wire stem. Would it not have been better to have danced the entire dance with a simple wire? The question is worth examining. (*OLF*, 281)

So far removed are Genet's writing and aethetics from the austerity of a simple wire stem that it can only be playfully that he questions the value of artifice, yet the presence of this expression of doubt at the end of *Our Lady of the Flowers* is no doubt a reminder of the tangled web of opposites that inhabit his texts.

2

The Flower of Their Strength

> The only live things I had ever owned were lovely pricks,
> whose roots were buried in black moss. I cherished several such,
> and I wanted them all in the flower of their strength.
> —*The Thief's Journal*

BEYOND THE BINARY

As mentioned on several occasions earlier, Sartre's *Saint Genet*
—however illuminating overall—does very little justice to what, after
all, is no small issue: the erotic dynamics at play in Genet's work. In
fact, one might say that this area constitutes Sartre's main blind spot.
Repeatedly, relentlessly, on what is a complex and fluid interplay of
relations, he imposes the fixity of an ultraconventional model of
male homosexual sex: one where there are two partners, one "active"
and one "passive," and one act, penetration (oral and/or anal), performed by the active partner onto (into) the passive one. Historians
and critics, from Michel Foucault to David Halperin, have traced
back to the Greeks this particular understanding and representation
of sexual relations in terms of activity and passivity and have shown
that, in such a model, the active role is consistently taken to reflect a
position of social domination and the passive one a position of social
submission as well as femininity.

To this classical, conventional model Sartre adds two other elements that reinforce its binary, oppositional structure. First, he often
suggests that the active and passive roles are fixed not only within a
relationship but within a lifetime, and it is almost obsessively that he
refers to Genet's *passive* homosexuality, as though it were a constant,

essentially defining feature. In *Saint Genet*, he restricts his textual examples to passages that reflect the fixity of his model and what he assumes to be the author's position within it. Furthermore, Sartre
offers an erroneous account of the distribution of pleasure which, he
claims, remains the privilege of the active partner only; the pleasure
of the passive partner is never sought nor received. Since it is not for
the sake of pleasure, then, why subject oneself to penetration, Sartre
asks, what is there to be gained? The answer he gives shows how
clearly his model of homosexuality replicates his understanding of
heterosexuality, for, as pointed out in the introduction, it simply re-
peats theories put forth by Simone de Beauvoir in *The Second Sex*
when she asks the same question of women and suggests the following answer: the passive partner steals the active partner's being in
order to incorporate it into himself.[1]

Sartre's insistence on the fixity of Genet's passive role is particularly odd, for in areas outside the erotic he very well understands and
praises precisely the opposite attitude: Genet's ability to fluctuate
from one pole to another. Sartre explains, for example, that the brilliant tension in Genet's work occurs because "[Genet] wants to do
and to be, to be in order to do and to do in order to be, *he is, at one
and the same time, the master, the slave, and their merciless struggle*" (*SG*,
126, my emphasis). Such an ability to assume oppositional roles in
the sexual arena, alternatively if not simultaneously, is quite evident
in *A Thief's Journal*, where the narrator describes his lover, the much-
admired Stilitano, in the following terms: "I was the beloved of such
a beautiful bird of prey" (*TJ*, 94). This certainly suggests that the narrator in this instance adopted a conventional passive role.[2] Nonetheless, the opposite role is described when he is with another, younger
lover: "We pulled off a few jobs and I became his master" (*TJ*, 93).
When further on in the novel he meets Armand, the narrator was
"dominated by his age and strength" and was "subjected to his pleasure" (*TJ*, 134). Again, this suggests a conventional passive role. Elsewhere in the same book, writing about yet another lover, Java, he tells
us: "When I buggered this handsome twenty-two year old athlete for
the first time he pretended to be sleeping" (*TJ*, 104). Here, the narrator is clearly active in his sexual relations. Similarly, many passages
in *Funeral Rites* suggest that the narrator can, and does, assume an active role (as well as a passive one) which is quite precisely described
throughout the passages detailing sex with the young Jean Decarnin
and clearly suggested when he talks about "the veneration I feel for

that part of the body [the anus] and the great tenderness that I have bestowed on the children who have allowed me to enter it, the grace and sweetness of their gift, oblige me to speak of all this with respect" (*FR*, 21).

In a footnote to the first few lines of *A Thief's Journal*, where he draws unlikely parallels between flowers and convicts, Genet writes: "My excitement is the oscillation from one to another" (*TJ*, 7). Clearly, this movement between opposed poles is something that he cultivates in the erotic realm as well—and so do characters other than the narrator. During the first encounter in *Funeral Rites*, between the German soldier Erik and the executioner (an older man and of a higher rank in the German army), it is the latter who, following conventional expectations, plays the active role: "The executioner was the first to break away, for he had discharged between Erik's golden thighs, which were velvety with morning mist" (*FR*, 71). Later, however, "the executioner had [Erik] play the male role in bed" (*FR*, 82). It is also quite obvious that, contrary to what Sartre claims, pleasure is not restricted to whom he terms the active partner and that often, as in the following passage, where the narrator sodomizes Java, pleasure is there for both:

> We form one body, but it has two heads and each of them is involved in experiencing its own pleasure . . . . I know that he derives this pleasure from me, that he awaits it from my hand that is jerking him off, but I feel that the only thing that concerns him now is his coming. (*TJ*, 105)

It would be repetitious to give further examples demonstrating the fallacy of Sartre's view and showing that, on the contrary, Genet's fiction offers ample evidence of relationships that allow for a fluctuation, rather than a fixity, of erotic roles and for the circulation, rather than the confinement, of pleasure. In fact, the erotics in these texts correlate with Kaja Silverman's suggestion, in *Male Subjectivity at the Margins*, that such fluctuations are likely to occur in a homosexual context: "Reversibility between subject and object would seem to me to come into play with particular facility within those fantasmatics that are predicated upon predominantly narcissistic object choices."[3]

While the passages quoted above clearly show that Genet's fiction offers many powerful alternatives to what Sartre viewed as the only possible model of homosexual relations, one cannot deny that replicas of heterosexual norms also exist in his work. Yet, in many instances, the surface appearance of conventionality is deceiving, and, in more or less subtle ways, the mimicry is not without simultaneously undermining that which on the surface it seems to uphold. For example, the couple that the drag queen Divine and the thief Darling form in many ways replicates the stereotypes of a conjugal one. She adores him, worships him, and he, eventually, falls in love with her. He becomes her pimp, she works for him while he goes to the movies, then he takes her out among his friends. She settles into "her married woman's happiness." Genet calls Divine and Darling "the ideal couple" (*OLF*, 93) and depicts their domestic coziness:

> In that big Montmartre attic . . . Darling will soon bring the midnight-blue overalls that he wears on the job, his ring of skeletal keys and his tools, and on the little pile which they make on the floor he will place his white rubber gloves, which are like gloves for formal occasions. Thus began their life together in that room through which ran the electrical wires of the stolen radiator, the stolen radio, and the stolen lamps. They eat breakfast in the afternoon. During the day, they sleep and listen to the radio. Toward evening, they primp and go out. (79)

This idealization of the conjugal, or, at least, references to it (and therefore to heterosexuality) as a norm, occurs also, although much more fleetingly, in *The Thief's Journal*. Genet writes of beggars where "the more loving of the two would say to the other: 'I'll take the basket this morning'" (*TJ*, 8). Elsewhere, the narrator claims that he is particularly proud of being with the handsome Stilitano because he imagines that he is the envy of women: "When I walk along the street, I wondered, am I being envied by the loveliest and wealthiest of Senoritas" (*TJ*, 58).

Yet the upholding of conjugal norms is far from absolute; in fact, many heterosexual patterns and institutions are derided. In Divine's and Darling's household, the coziness is disrupted by the presence of the tube of Phenobarbital on the mantelpiece, for example, which "detaches the room from the stone block of the building to suspend it like a cage between heaven and earth" (*OLF*, 79): with their connotations of suicide or murder, the barbiturates separate Divine's and Darling's domestic haven from others. Later, we are told that to be "neighborly" (by which one might understand wifely, conventional, unthreatening, good-hearted) Divine reads *Détective magazine*, a popular tabloid. But her understanding of neighborliness is not everyone's: her model is "Saint Catherine of Siena, who passed the night in the cell of a man condemned to death, on whose prick her head rested" (*OLF*, 93). Such subversions are not restricted to the passages that recount this relationship. A wedding ceremony had delighted Divine, when she was younger and still the village boy Louis Culafroy. He was quite taken by the charm of the sugared almonds, the white tulle, the wax orange blossoms. His attention, however, swiftly shifted away from such niceties when he noticed the priest's sprinkler that blessed the rings: "The sprinkler is always moist with a tiny droplet, like Alberto's prick which is stiff in the morning and which has just pissed" (*OLF*, 170). Similarly, nuptials are both upheld and subverted in the following lines from *Funeral Rites*:

> I loved [Riton]. I was going to marry him. It would perhaps be enough for me to be dressed in white for the wedding, though with a decoration of large black crepe cabbage rosettes at the ankles, the neck, the waist, the throat, the prick and the anus. Would Riton accept me dressed that way in a bedroom decked with irises? (*FR*, 58)

On other occasions, heterosexual norms are undermined not by the grotesque, as above, or by the intrusion of a stiff prick, as in the previous example, but by the suggestion that a *social* behavior that replicates a heterosexual one does not necessarily mean that the ensuing *erotic* behavior will do the same. In the following *rêverie*, the narrator adorns soldiers dancing at a Foreign Legion ball with the conventional charms and trimmings of a wedding ceremony (chaste, smile, rings, "I do") officiated by an imaginary priest:

> Though their dance was chaste at the beginning of Ramona, would it remain so when, in our presence, they wedded by exchanging a smile, as lovers exchange rings? To all the injunctions of an invisible clergy the Legion answered "I do." Each of them was the couple wearing both a net veil and a dress uniform (white leather, scarlet and green shoulder braid). They haltingly exchanged their manly tenderness and wifely modesty. To maintain the emotion at a high pitch, they slowed up and slackened their dance, while their pricks, numbed by the fatigue of a long march, recklessly threatened and challenged each other behind a barricade of rough denim. (*TJ*, 34)

The description appears at first to be organized along clearly gendered lines (the veil and the wifely modesty on the one hand, the uniform and the manly tenderness on the other). However, it becomes clear that both masculine and feminine are present within each person ("each of them was the couple") and that both soldiers actively engage each other sexually ("their pricks . . . recklessly challenged and threatened each other") rather than maintain active/passive, penetrator/penetrated divisions.

As well as undermining the heterosexual norms it simultaneously appears to uphold, Divine's and Darling's relationship is particularly interesting in that it challenges the unexamined acceptance of the organization of activity and passivity according to the criterion of penetration. Genet does not depict sex between Divine and Darling in very much detail, but it is quite clear that, in terms of Sartre's model, Divine is the passive one. However, a crucial point is the following: even though it is she who is penetrated, it is nonetheless from Divine that erotic initiatives, animation and energy flow, whereas Darling, the solid one, is also the inert one. The mechanism is well demonstrated in the following description of Darling's return to the garret: each time "Divine leaps to the assault, clings to her man, licks him and envelops him. He stands there, solid and motionless, as if he were Andromeda's monster changed to rock in the sea" (*OLF*, 86). Divine, in fact, is often characterized by her intense and constant movement: "She curls like a shaving from a turning lath . . . she twists her lithe white arms, rolls and unrolls them . . . " (*OLF*, 149). This much is constant in her relationship to the pimp: she is the one who unbuttons flies, who pulls up shirts. Darling's impassivity is always stressed: "Darling dances the java with his hands in his pockets. If he lies down, Divine sucks him" (*OLF*, 84). Dancing with his hands in his pockets, Darling projects self-containment, insulation, reticence, slight insolence; when he is still, Divine takes the initiative, and to some extent takes control of the situation. In the following lines, addressed to an unspecified "you," the utter immobility of the penetrator is emphasized:

> You did not move, you were not asleep, you were not dreaming, you were in flight, motionless and pale, frozen, straight, stretched out stiff on the flat bed like a coffin on the sea, and I know that we were chaste, while I, all attention, felt you flow into me, warm and white, in continuous little jerks. (*OLF*, 54)

The preceding examples show erotic dynamics emphasizing the activity of the person who conventionally would be characterized as passive, and depict the inertia of the one that Sartre would call active. Elsewhere in *Our Lady*, distinctions between motion and stillness, penetrator and penetrated, active and passive are very much blurred. There is, for example, an interesting reversal in the interplay of inertia and movement in the following lines where, furthermore, the image of penetration set up in the first part of the sentence is undone in the second and replaced by one of envelopment: "He rams it in so hard and calmly that anuses and vaginas slip onto his member like rings on his finger" (*OLF*, 106). Although on a metaphorical level, the next example suggests a symbiosis of sorts, a flow of "vigor" from the penetrator to the penetrated: "Smiles and sneers, alike inexorable, enter me by all the holes I offer, their vigor penetrates and erects me" (*OLF*, 54). Also reversed, in the following sentence, is the symbolism conventionally associated with guns. In a fantasy that stands out sharply in *Funeral Rites* because it appears quite disconnected from the rest of the narrative, the narrator shoots and kills a young child. As he holds the gun, it is not the obvious phallocentric connotations that surface (penetration, activity, aggression) but one suggesting receptivity (with the term "orifice") and, astonishingly, discourse (with the expression "having its say"): "I felt that the gun was becoming an organ of my body, an essential organ whose black orifice, which was marked by a more gleaming little circle, was, for the first time being, my own mouth, which was at last having its say" (*OLF*, 107). Finally, the idea of penetration and of a division of erotic roles is completely absent in the following description, still from *Our Lady of the Flowers:*

> Loving each other like two young boxers who, before separating, tear off each other's shirt, and when they are naked, astounded by their beauty, think they are seeing themselves in a mirror . . . and embrace each other like two young wrestlers (in Greco-Roman wrestling), interlock their muscles in the precise connections offered by the muscles of the other, and drop to the mat until their warm sperm, spurting high, maps out on the sky a milky way where other constellations which I can read take shape. (*OLF*, 89)

Rather than the interplay of opposition, the guiding principle in the above description is one of symmetry, of mirror image. Replacing the phallic concentration of sexual energy and activity, it is the entire body that through the curves of the muscles connects with the other, and sperm, rather than being confined to one orifice (there is no penetration here), reaches cosmic heights. The emphasis, here, on the complementarity of identical bodies makes this description most removed from heterosexual norms and the celebratory tone renders it the closest to contemporary homosexual utopias.

In earlier examples of erotic dynamics in Genet (who does what to whom) there were instances of replicas of heterosexual constructs, social and sexual, in nonheterosexual frameworks. Such replicas raise questions similar to those posed by drag and have provoked similar critical reactions. The most interesting and relevant among these seems best encapsulated in points made by Leo Bersani in "Is the Rectum a Grave?" on the one hand and in the analysis put forth by Judith Butler in *Gender Trouble* on the other.[4] Bersani is suspicious of such replicas. He suggests that they are viewed differently from within and without the group and that heterosexuals probably consider the homosexual adoption of conventional roles, living situations, etc., as a yearning for a patriarchal order. In other words, the adherence to conventional roles and values expresses what is misread as a complicity. Butler argues (and I will not repeat in detail ideas already discussed in the chapter on drag) that the counterdeployment of heterosexual constructs in a gay context denaturalizes them, shows their utterly constructed nature. To this one might add Foucault's general point that dominance is better challenged from inside, rather than from outside, the discursive framework on which it is founded. Although both positions appear valid, it seems likely that in Genet, the misreading that Bersani talks about is less likely to occur since the reader is offered an "inside view" of such constructs: the reader sees how the conventional aspects of Divine's and Darling's relationship are challenged by extremely nonconventional, indeed subversive, elements. The effect Genet's work most forcefully achieves, as far as this particular aspect of erotic relations is concerned, is one of denaturalization (such will not be the case for other aspects of erotic relations). Genet's texts challenge the very foundation of the conventional model whereby penetration is associated with activity and receptivity with passivity. These texts undo what is usually construed as an inevitable polarization and naturalization. To persist in calling "active" those whose bodies are characterized by reticence, stillness and inertia and "passive" those whose bodies display erotic movement and initiative, as does Sartre, is to reaffirm the intrinsic mastery of the phallus and to view its receptacle as the intrinsic locus of subordination. Genet does not go so far as to depict an erotic realm where oppositions, divisions, power differentials are negated; he does not suggest a utopic space such as that which Dennis Altman in *The Homosexualization of America* describes as "a sort of Whitmanesque democracy . . . far removed from the male bondage of rank, hierarchy and competition."[5] Yet Genet does to a significant extent subvert, complicate, recast oppositional categories and the dominant model of sexual and gender positionality, a subversion that is perhaps most effectively encapsulated in the following lines which challenge the old and deeply ingrained association of femininity in male homosexuality with youth and weakness: "To invent the woman. It is not the weaker, or the younger, or the more gentle of the two who succeeds better in this, but the one who has the more experience in it, frequently the stronger and older man" (*Q,* 126).

The present chapter, exploring an erotics far more complex than Sartre acknowledges, addresses a number of dissonances similar to the one suggested above. The first section will concern itself with the paradoxical situation whereby even though, in Genet's novels, the feminine is the most highly praised style, expressions of erotic desire are generally addressed to solid and tangible male bodies. Such bodies, however, are not without their evanescent side, as they sometimes fade into a haze. In the second section, turning my attention to the actual erotic dynamics (who does what to whom), I will show that they are fluid and open to reversals, that they have a destabilizing effect and allow the possibility of interactions beyond the fixed, bipolar oppositional model that Sartre proposes: a model that establishes an impermeable division between the "toughs" (the active homosexuals) and the "softs" (the passive homosexuals) and whereby sex organizes itself around the penetration of the one by the other according to a conventional heterosexual model.[6] In the last section I address the representation, role, and resonances of the phallus.

MUSCULAR MATERIALITIES

Although this analysis of the sexual politics in Genet significantly differs from Kate Millett's, there is truth to her remark that Genet has reserved intelligence and moral courage for his queens.[7] Divine, whom Millett views as "the most splendid character in his novels" (another very true point), is without any doubt the most striking embodiment of such qualities as well as the most brilliantly seductive and grippingly tragic. She is a character whose fluctuating range of emotions Genet depicts at length, providing her with what in conventional terms one might name "psychological depth," accentuated by the fact that *Our Lady of the Flowers* allows for detailed accounts of episodes in Divine's childhood and, in particular, of Louis's fraught relationship to his mother. Along with her intelligence, her courage, Divine's splendid performance of the feminine is worshipped throughout the novel: her gestures, her voice, her "charm, which emerges from her eyes" (*OLF*, 72)—all discussed in the previous chapter. What needs to be examined now is the body— flesh and bones—a body that, although not prominent and certainly not validated as constituting a "true" self, is not completely absent.

The most obvious aspect of Divine's naked body is that it is not represented as attractive. On the contrary, on the first of the few occasions when it is spoken of, it is in contrast to the firmness of her lover Gorgui's. The all-encompassing characteristic of hers is softness: "Everything about Divine is soft. . . . Divine is she-who-is-soft. That is, whose character is soft, whose cheeks are soft, whose tongue is soft, whose member is supple" (*OLF*, 179). No erotic sparks fly from this description nor from the following one where Divine expresses self-loathing:

> That evening, undressed and alone in the garret, she saw with fresh eyes her white, hairless body, smooth and dry, and in places, bony. She was ashamed of it, and hastened to put out the lamp, for it was the ivory body of Jesus on an eighteenth-century crucifix, and relationships with the divinity, even a resemblance to it, sickened her. (*OLF*, 135)

Suggested in both passages—with the softness in the first description, the white brittleness in the following one—is a body drained of blood and vitality. It is never presented, in and of itself, as an object of desire. It is clearly not in her flesh, in her anatomy, that Divine's seduction lies. In fact, in the following passage, her unadorned physique, stripped of its feminine accoutrements, is shown as something that Darling must overcome:

Many a time he had helped Divine fasten her wig on. His movements
had been skillful and, if I may say so, natural. He had learned to love
that kind of Divine. He had steeped himself in all the monstrosities
of which she was composed. He had passed them in review: her very
white dry skin, her thinness, the hollow of her eyes, her powdered
wrinkles, her sliced down hair, her gold teeth. He said to himself that
that's how it was. (*OLF*, 155)

Here, too, there is something cadaverous about Divine's body. In fact,
it is as though—though she is not yet dead—her flesh is already erod-
ing: her thinness, the hollowness of her eyes. There are also connotations, in this description, of a mummified corpse, with the dry skin,
the powder, the gold: a shell-like body, then, emptied of its flesh, of
its organs, and completely void of any erotic charge. What Genet calls
Divine's implacable seduction has little to do with her corporeal body
but rather with the performance of a highly stylized feminine self.

While Genet's work does not generally lend itself to classifications
and tends to resist oppositional models, when it comes to the gender
constitution of his characters, it is possible, without undue simplifi-
cation, to place Divine at the extreme feminine pole of the spectrum. On the other end is a particular type of masculinity that the
following pages will address, a masculinity characterized by the muscular materiality of bodies. This type of masculinity, of which bulk,
power and vigor are the most highly praised qualities, graces a number of characters in Genet's novels and is always erotically charged.
For example, in a fantasy of sex with a German executioner during
World War II, the (French) narrator of *Funeral Rites* imagines: "The
mere bulk of the man crushed me. I could tell that under his clothes,
under his open shirt, was a terrific mass of muscles" (*FR*, 37). In
Querelle, the sight of Norbert (a brothel keeper) and Mario (a police-
man) has the following effect on the sailor:

The outlines of their two bodies met to form one continuous pattern
and this seemed to blend their muscular bodies as well as their faces.
Seized by vertigo in the presence of these powerful muscles and
nerves that he perceived as towering above him—as one might when
throwing one's head back to appraise the height of a giant pine
tree—that kept on doubling and merging again, crowned by Mario's
beauty but dominated by Norbert's bald head and bullish neck,
Querelle stood there with his mouth half-open, his palate a little dry.
(*Q*, 30)

On a symbolic level, the thrill is at the merging of opposites (of outlaw and keeper of the law) while on a material level it is the fusion of the two massive bodies ("muscular," "powerful," "towering," "giant," "bullish") that has the overwhelming effect on the young and (as yet) inexperienced Querelle. Later in the same novel, when Querelle reflects further upon Mario, he continues to dwell upon the "thickness of his arms. The width of his shoulders" (*Q*, 37); and, in Norbert, he recognized "the authority in the man's thighs and chest, the sobriety of movement that endows a man with total power" (*Q*, 31). In *Our Lady of the Flowers*, as Darling makes his splendid appearance at Divine's funeral, the attending queens are in awe of "the weighty magnificence of the barbarian" and the manner in which "the torso on his hips was a king" (*OLF*, 59). Often praise and desire are lavished on a single body part—here a frightening neck, there a majestic back, later vigorous thighs—but it does not appear that one part of the body is overall privileged over another, with the exception, of course, of the phallus. An image that does recur throughout is that of a body part either emerging from or being perceptible under cloth, and, as is the case with the conventionally feminine erotics of veiling, concealing and revealing flesh, the cloth draws attention to, indeed emphasizes, the underlying material body and, in this case, the hardness of muscles: an "unyielding chest beneath the shiny satin of a jacket" (*OLF*, 137), a "frightening neck which emerged from a blue shirt" (*FR*, 16) or "corduroy pants setting off the buttocks" (*OLF*, 171).

One remembers Divine's gestures, sometimes light and fluttery, sometimes curvaceous and grandiose—but always, always profuse. The masculine bodies, on the other hand, display self-restraint. At most, they might strike a single pose, for example the following one shared by Gorgui and Alberto:

> [Gorgui] stood firm and straight, though leaning slightly back, motionless and solid, in the position of a kid who braces himself on his nervous knees to piss against nothing at all, or in the pose in which, you will recall, Lou discovered Alberto (Colossus of Rhodes), the most virile pose of sentinels: thighs spread, and their bayonet-guns, which they grip with both hands, planted smack between their boots, right up to their mouths. (*OLF*, 165)

When these men move, their motion is forward, straight ahead, their attitude impassive, in stark contrast to the agitated queens, as in the following passage showing Darling's arrival at Divine's funeral:

As he passed—the motion was revealed by an imperceptible movement of the torso—within themselves, secretly, Milord, the Mimosa,
Castagnette, in short, all the queens, imparted a tendril-like movement to their bodies and fancied they were enlacing this handsome
man, were twining about him. Indifferent and bright as a slaughter-
house knife, he passed by, cleaving them all into two slices which
came noiselessly together again, though emitting a slight scent of
hopelessness which no one denied. (*OLF*, 61)

In the description of these men's walks, terms suggesting nobility,
solemnity and self-assurance recur. Attention is also drawn to a contrast between the upper and lower body, as in "Darling of the noble
bearing, of the swaying hips, of the motionless shoulders" (*OLF*, 80)
or "the power of [Stilitano's] shoulders, the mobility of his buttocks"
(*TJ*, 121) resulting in a combination of groundedness and controlled
suppleness—but without agitation. An interplay between stillness
and, again, a very deliberate, very restrained motion is suggested
when, in the German soldier Erik, the narrator observes "the mobile
yet vigorously immobile legs of the compass which his legs were when
he walked." Connoted by the image of the compass is a rotation, a
turning on an axis, which is also present in this description of Armand: "Still leaning, he pivoted on his axis as a single block like the
gates of a temple" (*TJ*, 203).[8]

Prevalent in the representations of these men's bodies, as well as
in the accounts of how they move, is the suggestion of a certain
groundedness, of the pull of gravity, of a dense materiality. Beneath
this dense materiality is emptiness. In the previous chapter I argued
against the existence, in the queens, of an internal gender core, but
they were nonetheless rich in emotions, moral fiber—what Millett
calls their soul. The men, in comparison, appear as generally un-
thinking automats; they exist primarily as tangible flesh. Genet
points out their utter vacuity when at the beginning of *Our Lady of the
Flowers*, the narrator tells how, in jail, he cuts handsome, empty-eyed
heads out of magazines:

I say vacant, for all eyes are clear and must be sky-blue, like the razor's
edge to which clings a star of transparent light, blue and vacant, like
the windows of buildings under construction, through which you can
see the sky from the window on the opposite wall. (*OLF*, 52)

The discussion of Genet's representation of male bodies, up to
this point, seems to have underscored a clear distinction between the

feminine as style and the masculine as substance. However, things are rarely that simple with Genet, and the old dichotomy between the material and the immaterial has not yet resurfaced. Indeed, what one might call a haloed effect often derealizes these solidly material bodies, blurring their outlines, rendering them hazy, working against the impression of impermeability and self-containment they otherwise convey. Sometimes this halo can be created by a physical characteristic itself as when, in *Querelle*, Seblon delights in the sight and feel of his own legs, noting that "their black, strong hairs are quite soft in spite of their vigorous growth, and thus they create a kind of mist from foot to groin, which softens the roughness and stoniness of his muscles" (*Q*, 9). On other occasions, this softening of harsh contours is created by interactions with the external world, in this case a misty morning, and a vapor is seen as radiating from the body: "It was also as if the morning mist were a steady emanation from his extraordinarily powerful body, a body strong with such glowing life that the combustion caused that motionless, thick, and yet luminous white smoke to seep out through all its pores" (*FR*, 7). Elsewhere, an emotion, anger, takes on a tangible form to derealize the contours of the bodies of the "thieves and pimps" who "bent [the narrator] to their will"; in *The Thief's Journal*, he notes that "there escaped from them through the eyes, the nostrils, the mouth, the palm of the hand, the bulging basket through the brutal hillcock of the calf under the wool or denim, a radiant and somber anger, visible as a haze" (*TJ*, 14). In this final example, the process is taken one step further: the material body extends as shadow to derealize the world:

> To love a man is not only to let myself be excited by some of the details which I call nocturnal because they create within me a darkness wherein I tremble (the hair, the eyes, a smile, the thumb, the thigh, the bush, etc.) but also to make these details render as shadow everything possible, to develop the shadow of a shadow, hence to thicken it, to extend its realm and throng it with darkness. (*TJ*, 199)

Here, apart from noting the impact of certain tangible body parts upon him, the narrator comments on their effect on the world: to render as shadow everything possible. This effect is initially one of de-substantialization, for a shadow reveals only the outline of an object (rather than its matter) and a possibly distorted outline at that. With the development of "the shadow of a shadow" the process goes

one step further, the intensification of the shadow, a further derealization (and of course a physical impossibility).

As discussed in the previous chapter, gender in Genet is not completely unified. Even the more masculine characters often include,
in their attitude or occupation, an attribute that feminizes them. Remembering that the main characteristic of Divine's body is her softness, the preceding example of Seblon's delight at how the hairs on
his leg soften the otherwise harsh outline of his muscles suggests that
this feminization can also be located in some instances of the erosion
of bodily contours, and that it is a pleasurable experience. Elsewhere, the interplay is less between masculine and feminine than between material and immaterial, as when the halo is seen as the
consequence of a combustion within, indicating both the creation of
energy and the destruction of substance. When anger escapes as a
haze through the calves (as well as, more conventionally, through the
eyes and nostrils), the suggestion is of a porous body rather than one
that is mineral and impermeable. Interestingly, what all these examples have in common is this: the destabilization of bodily contours—
something noted earlier in a very different phenomenon, drag. In
drag, the contours of the body can be destabilized through surgery,
hormones or "props" such as wigs, nails, breasts. Here, while these
masculine bodies are not made of pieces, as Genet says about those
of his queens, their boundaries can be unexpectedly precarious
nonetheless. While clearly it occurs on a more literary than literal
level, the process of effacement works to undo the otherwise conventional attributes of masculinity.

THE PHALLUS

In the last section of *Male Subjectivity at the Margins*, Kaja Silverman
offers a brilliant analysis of the erotics in Proust's *Remembrance of
Things Past*, demonstrating how this work invites us to conceptualize
a male homosexuality within which the male organ does not play the
usual role as the primary site of male eroticism.[9] Proust's texts work
against the assumption that male homosexuality necessarily implies
"only penises and anuses, or penises and mouths." It would certainly
be helpful to a feminist assessment of Genet if one could say the
same thing about his novels; unfortunately one cannot. Even the
most perfunctory reading of his work reveals that the male genitals

are the primary source and locus of excitement, suggesting at first sight a homosexuality based on a narcissistic attraction to the phallic attributes of the other. This, however, does not say it all, and a closer look at how these phallic attributes are represented in Genet's work, how they function and what they mean, will bring to light erotic dynamics more complex and ambiguous than one might at first imagine. While one cannot say of Genet's work the same as Silverman says of Proust's—that it displaces what she calls "the premium which male homosexuality places on the male sexual organ"—there are other significant elements that differ from, and even perhaps challenge, dominant paradigms.

There are a number of conventional aspects to Genet's representation of the phallus which must first be taken into account. I showed earlier that in his *Saint Genet* Sartre offered an overly simple reading of sexual activity and passivity. When he talks about the representation and role of the sex organ in Genet's texts (and in Genet's own sexuality, for he constantly conflates the two), though he again oversimplifies the issue, there is some validity to his comment: "What excites Genet about a prick is never the flesh of which it is composed, but its power of penetration, its mineral hardness." Indeed, Sartre is correct in saying that the penis of flesh and blood—the penis of porn movies, realistically represented—is not what Genet is interested in depicting. Also true is the fact that, on many occasions, its matter, its substance is described in mineral terms: "an erect penis, stony beneath the silk" (*OLF*, 137), "a heavy prick, as polished and warm as a column in the sun" (*OLF*, 127), "the violent member turned to stone" (*OLF*, 233). Further, as is typical of many of Genet's images (in fact, of his aesthetics in general, as by now must be evident), those representing the penis often bring together opposed terms, as in the following, where the organic (algae), the mineral (stone) and a hybrid of both (shellfish) are combined in one image: "His member and its surrounding bush suddenly seemed to him to be a kind of stone at the bottom of the sea, encrusted, among the algae, with tiny shellfish that made it even harder" (*FR*, 92).

Another conventional aspect of his representation of the penis is that of the disembodied organ, depicted as quite separate from the rest of the anatomy, endowed with an existence, life, presence of its own. Such was the case in the image of the penis made of stone at the bottom of the sea, and in the following one too, where the pricks, although taking root in the body, are shown to grow from it and achieve an existence of their own (the only live *things* I owned): "The only live things I have ever owned were lovely pricks, whose roots were buried in black moss" (*TJ*, 139). In *Our Lady of the Flowers*, Darling's is isolated from the torso through similar processes of idolization: "Divine takes care of his penis, caresses it with the most profuse tenderness. . . . She has beribboned the bush and penis, stuck flowers into the buttonholes of the fly" (*OLF*, 107). On other occasions, the phallus is given a preeminence of its own not through its objectification but through its designation as a locus of concentrated energy. Again, this is a fairly conventional representation. About Stilitano, in *The Thief's Journal*, the narrator raves: "All his brilliance, all his power had their source between his legs . . . he generated in the darkness of a well buttoned fly, though buttoned by only one hand, the luminosity with which its bearer will be aglow" (*TJ*, 25). Later, of sex with Armand, he writes: "All his muscles will be conscious, however, of being the tributaries of a virility converging at that hard and violently charged point" (*TJ*, 234). There is no doubt that in the instances described above, the imagery with which Genet depicts the male organ is far from banal. It is highly idiosyncratic and striking. Yet, in these instances as in many others, whether Genet depicts it as a stony, rigid instrument, brings it to life through animistic worship or imagines it as the locus of concentrated energy, the phallus is invested with conventional properties.

As is often the case with Genet, representations that clearly deviate from the norm occur alongside more traditional ones. For example, while it is usually the erect organ that is celebrated, the flaccid one is also cherished as in the following lines where it is simultaneously feminized. The episode from *Funeral Rites* occurs when Riton lies next to Erik, both fully clothed. He becomes obsessed with the thought of Erik's penis and seeks it out in the dark:

> Finally [his fingers] felt a warm, soft mass. . . . They very delicately tried to distinguish the various parts of that mass whose abandon in his hands gratified him . . . with the skill of a lacemaker, the hand above the dark cloth was able to sort out the confusion of the treasure which lay there all jumbled up. I prejudged its splendor in action and imprisoned it, sleeping little girl that it was, in my big ogre's paw. I was protecting her. I weighed her in my hand and thought: "There's treasure in there." (*FR*, 154)

Further, along with this instance of its feminization, another image occurs very frequently: that suggesting a flowering, a blooming. Notwithstanding the fact that flowers are the reproductive organs of plants (and containing both the male and female organs), their connotations are rarely male or sexual; rather, flowers customarily suggest fragility, purity, ephemerality, etc., and their presence in the context of the representation of the phallus is highly unexpected. It is unexpected and pervasive. For example, in the following set of sentences, where the narrator in drag encounters a Gypsy in Spain, though the rapprochement is not clearly formulated, there is no doubt a resonance between the prick and the flowering almond trees: "I fell astride the Gypsy's prick. The flounces of my skirt covered the countryside like moss. It was April, and the moon lit up a vast stretch of flowering almond trees around Granada" (*FR*, 157). The comparison is made very clear in the following instance where, mourning his dead lover, the same narrator notes that "in my memory, his prick, which used to discharge so calmly, assumes the proportions and at times the serene appearance of a flowering apple tree in April" (*FR*, 218). Two things are suggested in the simile. First, the image of the flowering tree, remembered as serene, is invested with what one might think of as a behavioral component: gathered, calm, self-contained—rather than driven, as Sartre would have it, by its power of penetration. Second, the reference to the proportions of a tree hints at an opening up and curving of a vertical line (which, although exaggerated, is not anatomically incorrect), rendered even more precisely in the following example from *The Thief's Journal*, where the narrator muses upon his lover's penis: "From where could such a marvelous result (the flower crowning it is a lump of thistle) have been transplanted?" (*TJ*, 169). Also suggesting state of mind as well as appearance are the following lines from *Our Lady of the Flowers*, where much admiration is expressed for "the big inflexible pimps, members in full bloom—I no longer know whether they are lilies or whether lilies and members are not totally they" (*OLF*, 54). It is useful here to turn to the French expression for what Bernard Frechtman translated as "members in full bloom": *sexes épanouis*. Certainly, *épanoui* can refer to the blooming of flowers but also denotes a psychological (human) state of serenity, fulfillment, almost always applied to a woman, and, more often than not, referring to the effects of sexual/reproductive plenitude. The same word is used when Querelle, lying in bed at night, reflects upon his

own erection: "Cela, s'était l'ancien Querelle, affleurant, s'épan-
ouissant, montrant l'envers délicat de ses pétales" [He smiled: that
was the old Querelle, blooming, lightening up, showing the delicate
underside of his petals] (Q, 41). Again, blooming is the translation
of s'épanouir. One should also note, here, the term affleurer (mis-
translated as "lightening up"). It suggests the rising of an object
(usually to the surface of water)—denoting the moment, then, that
precedes the blooming. And, phonetically, affleurer is very close to
effleurer [to lightly touch]; embedded in both is the word fleur
[flower].[10]

Such floral imagery is not one that can in any way be construed to
convey a property that, according to Sartre, alone defines the penis:
its power of penetration. Earlier in this chapter I showed how penetration is not represented in the traditional terms of activity and passivity; how in Genet's texts it is generally the case that the one whose
penis finds itself in a mouth or anus remains impassive, while the
other, whose mouth or anus serves as receptacle, activates himself
around the very still body: "Anuses and vaginas slip onto his member
like rings on his finger." The predominant image is not of penetration but a quite different one: ensheathment. Along similar lines was
the earlier mention that it is always Divine who approaches Darling,
clings to him, envelops him, while he remains absolutely still. Also
relevant here is the passage from Funeral Rites where Erik (the German soldier) is asleep and Riton (from the French Militia) caresses
him, showing, again, the passivity of the one whose phallus is sought.
The episode continues, with the narrator now fantasizing that he is
Riton:

> Since my stroking had just given Erik a violent hard-on, he was
> awake, and he did not rebel. I waited wonderful moments, and it's
> amazing that there was not born of that waiting, from the moment
> that begins with the prick's awakening to happiness, the most fabu-
> lous of heroes, as Chrysaor sprang from the blood of Medusa, or new
> rivers, valleys, chimeras, in a leap on a bed of violets, hope itself in a
> white silk doublet with a feathered cap, a royal beast, a necklace of
> golden thorns, or tongues of flames, a new gospel, an aurora borealis
> over London or Frisco, a perfect sonata, or amazing that death itself
> did not make a fulgurant appearance between the two lovers. My
> hand squeezed the cock a second time; it seemed monstrously big.
>
> "If he sticks the whole caboodle up my cornhole he'll wreck the
> works." (FR, 155)

Here, too, there are many unconventional elements in Genet's representation of the phallus. The first and last two sentences of this passage refer to the material body in the most blunt and prosaic of terms; to the act of penetration in the most mechanistic ones; and to a common concern with a touch of base humor. Yet these sentences frame a lyrical explosion of highly literary images that sweep across time, place, mythologies and religion. It is the moment of phallic awakening (a transitional state, flesh passing from one sate to another, a metamorphosis of sorts) that is felt as sublime and brings on a wild flight of images that tumble, Rimbaldian, onto one another. These, however, contain little conventional erotic element; they harbor no traditional tropes of desire and derealize the physical, material reality in which they have their source, most ultimately with the expression of amazement that "death itself did not make an appearance." What we have here is the intimate co-existence, dissonant but not discordant, of the fantasized image and the tangible body, the basely denotative and the exquisitely connotative. Also unconventional is the fact that most exalted is the moment of phallic awakening rather than that of penetration which is referred to in a most unrefined manner ("stick up my cornhole"). And, throughout this entire episode, the one whose phallus is the source of such literary expansiveness lies completely motionless. This passage where Riton/the narrator caresses the fully clothed German soldier also contains a highly recurrent motif: that of an erect organ discernible under cloth.

Indeed, one of the most striking and deeply ambiguous aspects of Genet's erotics is the representation of what resonates with the Lacanian notion of the veiled phallus and brings further ambiguity to the erotic dynamics in these texts. This image, in Genet, is one of the most celebrated and the most sexually charged. As one drag queen plainly put it to another: "My dear, it's when the cuties still have their pants on that I like them" (*OLF*, 110). In *The Thief's Journal*, the narrator fondly remembers a scene where two Foreign Legion soldiers dance together, a dance at the end of which "their pricks . . . recklessly threatened and challenged each other behind a barricade of rough denim" (*TJ*, 34). A similar image operates when Divine, arrested by two policcmen, imagines that "their huge cocks are alive and rap sharply or push with desperate, sobbing thrusts against the door of their blue woolen pants" (*OLF*, 102). In these instances, the cloth offers a resistance, a screen that contains the erection. On

other occasions, the eroticism of the image is of a different order: it
stems from the contrast between the hardness of the organ and the
fluidity of a light, flimsy fabric.[11] Certainly, the impact of the bringing
together of opposed textures and consistencies is not without sensuality and such connection characterizes much of Genet's work. In an
image spoken of earlier, the young boy Louis Culafroy (who later was
to become Divine) imagines that "he would tenderly place his cheek
against an erect penis, stony beneath the silk" (OLF, 137). One of the
most memorable episodes, in the same novel, occurs when Our Lady
wears drag for the first time and the tight-fitting silk dress makes his
erection all the more noticeable, a "jutting horn that is raising the
silk" (OLF, 220).

These are just a few of the variations Genet plays on a highly recurrent motif. Such images are particularly noteworthy because of
their frequency and the high erotic charge they carry. Equally striking is their ambiguity: what we have here is a veil that removes from
immediate sight but does not entirely repress or conceal, a veil that
covers but nonetheless draws attention to the contours of the organ.
Signification parallels can be drawn between this image and Lacan's
notion of the veiled phallus, which he writes about in "The Significance of the Phallus." There, he maintains that it is precisely the veil
that confers to the phallus its ability to signify:

> The Phallus can play its role only when veiled, that is to say, as itself a
> sign of the latency with which any signifiable is struck, when it is
> raised to the function of signifier.[12]

This remark, describing the transformation of a material organ into
a signifier, is particularly interesting in light of another quote, taken
from the opening pages of Genet's The Thief's Journal:

> I wanted to call [the criminals] by charming names, to designate
> their crimes with, for modesty's sake, the subtlest metaphor (be-
> neath which veil I would not have been unaware of the murderer's
> rich muscularity, of the violence of his sexual organ). Is it not by the
> following image that I prefer to imagine them in Guiana: the
> strongest, with a horn, the "hardest," veiled by mosquito netting? (TJ,
> 10).

The main point in the first sentence echoes Lacan's: Genet suggests
a connection between signifying ("charming names," "subtlest meta-

phor") and the veiled phallus. Yet in the parentheses of this first sentence—parentheses that, like the veil, have the dual function of repressing while drawing attention to what it contains—Genet points out that the cloth does not succeed in completely erasing the corporeal reality: "beneath which veil I would not have been unaware of . . . " In the last sentence, the veil no longer represents a linguistic function, but is re-literalized, invested with the materiality of a mosquito net—a flimsy materiality, perhaps, but precise—still, of course, wrapped around the "hardest" of erections. In this passage, the veiled phallus, while being brought to bear upon a realm of language and desire, remains nonetheless anchored to a solidly male body.

This slippage and equivocation between the relationship of the veiled phallus to sign and body becomes particularly interesting in light of Kaja Silverman's "The Lacanian Phallus," a piece that partakes in the feminist debate about whether there exists an essential link between the Lacanian phallus and the male anatomy.[13] There, she demonstrates that Lacan is not really successful in maintaining the separation between the penis (organ) and the phallus (signifier) and shows that his discussion of the veiled phallus is particularly symptomatic of this slippage. While, on the one hand, Silverman agrees with Lacan's point that "the phallic signifier can function only when withdrawn from sight" and that the veil suggests "the loss of immediacy which occurs when an object is transformed into a signifier," she argues that it is also the case that Lacan unveils the phallic signifier as a penile representation.[14] Indeed, Silverman demonstrates that while Lacan's discussion emphasizes the lifting of an object into signification (echoing Genet's reference to the veil as "charming name," "subtlest metaphor"), it does not ignore "the penile erection whose contours can still be made out beneath the veil" (echoing Genet's reference to "the hardest" beneath the mosquito net).[15]

The importance that both Genet and Lacan accord to the veiled phallus is striking, and the way in which Silverman reads this motif in Lacan is useful to a reading of Genet. The process is one whereby the veiling, while it to some extent derealizes the penis and elevates it to a realm of signification, is not without reinforcing its material reality. This type of ambiguity is one that exists in other aspects of Genet's representation of the male organ. As discussed earlier, the terms of that representation, though never realistic and lacking pornographic minutiae, often connote qualities with which it is invested in

2 / THE FLOWER OF THEIR STRENGTH

traditional, heterosexual contexts: such qualities—solidity, hardness, strength—imbue Genet's representation of the male body in general. These representations, however, must be viewed in conjunction with other very different ones, those of the blossoming organ which not only deflects the vertical line but also adds an aura of fragility and ephemerality. And even though the phallus is often invested with an active power of penetration, it is not unusual for it to be solid but inert, as Genet offers an erotic paradigm whereby the body that would traditionally be called passive does not submit to but wraps around the motionless other, envelops the hard phallus within itself. In Genet's erotic realm, then, opposed paradigms are brought together; as he put it in a footnote to *The Thief's Journal:* "My excitement is the oscillation from one to another" (*TJ,* 7). The motif of the veiled phallus operates in a similar manner, relying on a derealization of an organ that remains nonetheless perceptible. The conjunction of the material and the semiotic is perhaps best characterized by this final passage, taken from the last page of *Our Lady of the Flowers,* where embedded in the narrative is a letter that Darling, in jail, sends to Divine:

> . . . Remember the things we used to do together. Try to
> recognize the dotted lines. And kiss it. A thousand big
> kisses, sweetheart, from
> Your Darling

> The dotted line that Darling refers to is the outline of his prick. I once saw a pimp who had a hard-on while writing to his girl place his heavy cock on the paper and trace its contours. I would like that line to portray Darling. (*OLF,* 307)

And so ends the novel. Darling is reduced to this: to his penis literally inscribed in his text, with the most minimalist of signs, the dot, conveying, however, not an approximate, guessed-at rendering, but a precise though fragmented tracing—dependent on the organ's presence ("heavy") on the page.

Not unlike the manner in which muscular bodies are derealized by haloed effects, the phallus, with suggestions of curvature, metaphors of bloom and tropes of veiling, is often represented in conventional ways. Nonetheless, it is also shown in rather unconventional terms, as an entity of mineral hardness, quite separate from the rest of the body; and it is insistently present throughout Genet's novels. This insistent presence alone is enough to challenge the point made by Hélène Cixous in her essay "The Laugh of the Medusa" that these texts can be viewed as instances of *écriture féminine*. As mentioned in the "Introduction," some aspects of Genet's texts correspond with that notion: the ambiguities of meaning, the syntactic disruptions, the undoing of binary oppositions in the realm of gender and sexuality—but all of these features notwithstanding, the omnipresence of the phallus is impossible to reconcile with the idea of a specifically feminine text. At the same time, one might wonder whether the presence of the phallus automatically means that Genet's writing is phallocentric. I would suggest not: while these texts cannot be viewed as feminine, they cannot be viewed as phallocentric either, because they do not uphold a patriarchal social order. On the contrary, by disrupting what at first might appear as replicas of heterosexual models, Genet challenges such an order. Much of the analysis in this chapter sought to highlight such disruptions. To recapitulate certain key points: Genet defies the organization of an active/passive dichotomy where the active role is taken to reflect a position of social domination and the passive one a position of social submission; he opens up this model to fluctuations and reversals, often giving energy and movement to the one who is penetrated while the one with the phallus lies motionless. Concerning models of social behavior, there's the fact that visible on the mantelpiece of Divine's and Darling's otherwise cozy home, the tube of barbiturates casts a shadow over the atmosphere of domestic bliss; also in *Our Lady of the Flowers* the sacred moment of a nuptial mass where the priest blesses the wedding ring veers off course when the sprinkler of holy water is compared to Alberto's moist prick. Another actual wedding scene in *Funeral Rites* gives rise to the fantasy of a homosexual one where various body parts are adorned with black rosettes.

Yet, while Genet's texts more or less subtly deride heterosexual models, no alternative models are set up in their place, no gay utopias are proposed. On the contrary, what is privileged in Genet are moments and elements of uncertainty, fluctuation, oscillation, such elements that Gilbert and Gubar locate in female-authored representations of drag, and, as I discussed in the previous chapter, there are similarities between Genet's representations of cross-dressing and those of Woolf and Barnes, for instance. This aspect of Genet's novels is another that *Saint Genet* did not adequately address, for while Sartre occasionally recognized the power of a particular gender performance, he nonetheless maintained his belief in the existence of an internal gender core. His clusters of novels from the 1940s can hence be read in ways very different from those which Sartre suggested in 1952 and are surprisingly relevant to a number of theories and debates that animate the field of gender studies in the late twentieth century. Also relevant to contemporary concerns is Genet's relationship to the political realm, which the next two chapters will address.

3

The Shadow of a Gun

> But the world can be changed by other means than the sort of
> wars in which people die: power may be at the end of a gun, but
> sometimes it is at the end of the shadow or image of a gun.
> —"May Day Speech"

Towards Engagement

In the early days of May '68, Genet returned to Paris after a long journey through Asia. Walking with his friend Derrida through the streets of the city, streets already desolate and paralyzed by the onset of the revolt but strewn with black and red flags, he exclaimed: "Ah! how beautiful it is! how beautiful it is!"[1] Soon after, in a spirited defense of Daniel Cohn-Bendit, the widely recognized "porte parole" of the insurrection, Genet reiterated his delight. The following passage is from "Lenin's Mistresses," a piece published at the end of May in the centrist weekly *Le Nouvel Observateur*, and which can be viewed as Genet's first specifically political intervention in the press:

> The traveler who goes through Paris knows the sweetness and elegance of a city in revolt. The automobiles, which make up its fat, have disappeared. Paris has become a thin city, has lost a few kilos, and for the first time of his life, the traveler returning to France has the exhilaration and joy to see faces that he had known listless turn joyous and beautiful. If the days of May had produced only that, already.*
> (*ED*, 31)

The lines quoted above, which convey a reaction of an aaesthetic order (the pleasing effects of the revolt on the appearance and ambiance of the city) occur among Genet's arguments in defense of Cohn-Bendit after the young rebel had come under recent attack for his romantic liaison with the daughter of a high-ranking conservative government official (hence the title of the article: a reference to Lenin's bourgeois mistresses). Genet describes Cohn-Bendit as the brilliant *emmerdeur* (roughly translated as "pain in the ass") of the bourgeoisie, an expression that, if it does not suggest revolutionary efficacy, should nonetheless be taken as highly complimentary—on the part of this particular author. He writes approvingly of Cohn-Bendit's political analyses (which spring from a radical left-wing/anarchist tradition) and applauds his concrete demands: to give workers access to university cafeterias, to allow them to attend higher education classes three full days a week, for example. Further on in the article he goes so far as to suggest that the movement Cohn-Bendit heads is in the process of seriously destabilizing the ruling class, but, at the same time, makes clear in the passage quoted above that the renewal of the Parisian landscape would have been sufficient success.

In this early political piece, optimistic in tone, strategic in its support of the much maligned Cohn-Bendit, Genet praises both the political and aesthetic consequences of May '68. Two years later, however, after the sobering realization that the revolt failed to reap the much-hoped-for benefits, he expresses regrets in an interview with the German writer Hubert Fichte. While acknowledging the importance of the aaesthetic side of the rebellion, Genet strongly laments its political impotence. He explains that, in general, power cannot be dissociated from theatricality—that, in fact, power shields itself behind theatricality. However, the one place in the world where the theatrical does not conceal and protect power is, precisely, a theater. It was therefore a mistake, Genet argues, for the students to have occupied the Théatre de l'Odeon, a site of political inefficacy. It would of course have been more difficult to have occupied the Palais de Justice (the courthouse) he admits, since it is of course better secured than a theater, but the effort would have been worthwhile and the results far more valuable. There, the students would have been compelled to organize trials, issue prison sentences (rather than the utopic declarations on the stage of the Odéon), and one might have witnessed the beginning of a real revolution. Sadly, it did not happen, Genet concludes.

Surfacing from these early considerations about May '68 are the two types of reactions that reoccur throughout all of Genet's further writings on political issues: a delight expressed at the aaesthetics of revolutionary activity (the elegant city strewn with black and red flags) on the one hand and a recognition of the necessity for strategic actions on the other. These dual reactions are clearly present in an article about the 1968 Democratic Convention in Chicago which Genet had been asked to cover for the magazine *Esquire*.[2] Sitting out in Lincoln Park with William Burroughs, Allen Ginsberg (whom he later addressed as "my only sunshine, my only light in America")[3] and crowds of hippies, Genet was very much entertained and somewhat moved by the surrounding activity. As had May in Paris, this highly charged political moment, with its intense fusion of rebellion and celebration, seemed to rejuvenate him. Displaying amused and affectionate indulgence for Ginsberg's Buddhist chants, rejoicing at the public burning of draft cards, Genet also expressed some fondness for those he calls hippies, treating them with quite unexpected good humor and acquiescing to their request to step on stage and say a few words. While he writes that "this youth is beautiful and full of gentleness" he nonetheless regrets the hippies' lack of strategic thinking and remarks, for example, that the sleep-ins at Lincoln Park were an overly poetic response to the ugly politics going on inside the convention hall. He addresses them in the final lines of the article he wrote for *Esquire:*

> Wonderful hippies, it is to you that I address my final supplication: children, children covered in flowers from all over the world, to fuck over the old sons of bitches who make your life hell, unite yourself, go underground if necessary to rejoin the burnt children of Vietnam.* (*ED*, 319)

In the last line of the article, Genet advocates unity with the burnt children of Vietnam, and without any doubt, encourages the hippies to adopt a Socialist politics. This recognition that, the joyfulness and elegance of the revolt notwithstanding, political efficacy requires more classic revolutionary strategies is one that pervades his writing on both the Panthers and Palestinians. His advice to the hippies was not taken, of course, and later, in *Prisoner of Love*, Genet remembers and speaks of them in a far more critical manner than in 1968: "The hippies, covered in flowers and vague ornaments, made love and got stoned and sank" (*PL*, 213). It is precisely in opposition to their softness, formlessness and self-indulgence, to their descent "further and further into negation, sinking and fading uncontrollably into drugs"

(*PL*, 213), that he places the group to whom he would dedicate much of his time and writing, the Black Panthers: "But a rough Black movement, strict when need be, was trying to understand this world, this rejected world, in order to build another" (*PL*, 213). He notes that although they were not averse to style and emblems, the Panthers, unlike the pacifist hippies, were also reliant on guns and strategies, the willing to sacrifice their own lives: "The Black Panthers' Party, faced with that dive into the void, braced itself, used every means, deliberately used its own life if necessary, and raised this necessity around itself to endow the black race with form" (*PL*, 213).[4]

Perhaps because while in Chicago he had met members of the Black Panther Party who had talked to him about their persecution and hopes for the future, Genet's piece about the Democratic Convention contains several references to racial oppression, in particular to police brutality against Blacks. Sometime later, in February 1970, two Panthers contacted him in Paris and requested his support for their struggle, which had become the object of intense repression and the source of some concern on the American political scene. Genet immediately agreed. He later explained that his enthusiasm and availability were a direct consequence of the nostalgia he felt for the *esprit de mai* that had flourished in Paris two years earlier (*ED*, 41). Genet, then, flew to Canada and from there, as he had prior to the Democratic Convention, he entered the United States illegally. (Because of his prison record and his homosexuality the State Department refused to grant him a visitor's visa.) For three months he lived with a group of Panthers, traveled with them from university to university, spoke and wrote in their favor and enabled them to speak also in places to which they would otherwise have been denied access. He put his literary legitimacy at their service in the absence, he said, of an American of equal status and shared sympathies. To an audience of students and professors at Yale on 1 May 1968, he announced: "And I must admit that, up till now, in America, there has been no Clémenceau, no Jaurès, and especially, among the intellectuals, no Zola to write *J'Accuse*. A *J'Accuse* which would bear witness against the courts of your country and against the majority of whites who have remained racists" (*ED*, 51). By enabling the Panthers to gain access and be heard in academic contexts and to draw crowds perhaps larger and of a different social composition than they might otherwise have expected, Genet adopted what, in conventional marxist doctrine, is considered one of the useful functions of intellectuals: he allowed his prestige and legitimacy to reflect favorably upon a revolutionary group. He also fulfilled two other roles of the revolutionary intellectual: he acted as a political agitator by contributing to the organization, in France, of groups supporting the Black Panthers and working for the release of George Jackson and Angela Davis; and he wrote a number of important pieces that one might call political journalism.

Genet's writing on the Black Panthers fits into three categories. First, there's the cluster of speeches he gave on university campuses from March to July 1970, some of which were later published in the French and American press, then collected in the posthumously published and as-yet-untranslated *L'Ennemi déclaré*. In July 1970 he wrote what is perhaps his most widely read political piece: the preface to George Jackson's *Soledad Brother*, closely followed by a group of texts on Jackson's imprisonment, trial, and death. Many years later, and in a purely literary vein, among his recollections of the Palestinians in *Prisoner of Love*, he included nostalgic reminiscences of the time he spent at the Panthers' side. The following chapter will concern itself with the politics and aaesthetics of these various texts, which clearly differ from Genet's early work in an obvious way: though not altogether absent, considerations on gender and sexuality play a far lesser role than previously. In particular, the pursuit of phallic eroticism is much attenuated. Further, these texts offer a representation of women that is actually quite positive, and will become even more so in Genet's writing on the Palestinians. The two preceding chapters have shown that what is celebrated, in Genet's fiction, is a stylish and stylized performance of the feminine which has little to do with the much maligned "titty females" (*OLF*, 230). Women (biological women) are portrayed in a harsh manner most of the time (Ernestine in *Our Lady*, Jean's mother in *Funeral Rites*), and ambiguously at best (Lysiane in *Querelle*). However, when he talks of those who fought alongside the Panthers, or of Angela Davis whom he'd met when he spoke at UCLA in April 1970, it is in highly sympathetic terms. In fact, he wrote several pieces specifically in support of Davis when she was considered a fugitive of justice and after her arrest. In 1976, six years after his final word on the death of George Jackson, he took to the pen again, and in "The Tenacity of Black Americans" he reintroduced her to the French public (or a section thereof) in *L'Humanité*, the daily newspaper of the French Communist Party. Here, taking a step back from his earlier intense relationship with the Panthers, he paints a more general picture of the Civil Rights Movement and begins with the customary narrative of Rosa Parks, then moves on to Martin Luther King, Malcolm X, the Panthers, and finally Angela Davis whose allure reinforces his belief in the interrelation of poetry and revolution: "Her beauty illuminates the stage. Once more I am convinced that revolutions would be impossible without the poetry of individual revolts that precede it" (*ED*, 186). Eventually, the essay takes the form of a conversation between Davis and himself, an exchange of views and comments on the current and past situation of Blacks in America and, echoing the way in which it began, ends with Genet's expression of admiration for the struggle of Black women. Similarly, *Prisoner of Love* contains many expressions of admiration for those Palestinian women who fought alongside the fedayeen.

As for more general considerations on the erotic realm, Genet's political pieces avoid them altogether; the topic is broached in the pages of *Prisoner of Love* that concern the Panthers but in an unexpected manner. When he writes about the erotic play among them, it is to dismiss the impact of an obvious phallocentrism directed at the outside world and symbolized to some degree by the visible carriage of a gun. An ostentatious phallic exhibitionism is no doubt a reappropriation and intensification of a White obsession projected onto the Panthers, Genet suggests. More relevant and more interesting to him than the macho posturing that is largely in the eye of the beholder are more subtle erotic dynamics at play among the Panthers, vital interactions that guarantee the cohesion of the group: "In spite of their Korean retenue—North Korean—the Black Panthers could not help this: to attract each other, so that the Black Panther Party was made up of magnetized bodies magnetizing each other" (*PL*, 260). Among these bodies, Genet perceives the tension of contradictory forces, retenue and attraction; in their voices, he hears a double edge of violence and tenderness. As well as non-gender-specific, the sexual energy that pervades the group was extraordinarily fertile, he says: "True, there was a kind of mad fertility about it all. . . .The Blacks made you think of ferns, or tree-ferns, without flowers or fruit, whose perpetuation and repercussion occur with the bursting of spores" (*PL*, 292, *mod*). Perpetuation and repercussion, not reproduction: the male and female principles are not at play here. Perpetuation suggests an uninterrupted line into the future, that Genet comments on elsewhere: "May the absence and invisibility of the

Blacks we call dead be well understood: they remain activity or radio-activity" (*PL*, 218, *mod*). Repercussion connotes indirect, fragmented effects or reactions along a line that can be deflected, angled in relation to its source. We are far from a phallic sexuality here. When Genet further defines the effect of this eroticism, along with fluidity, dispersal, non-gender-specificity, he introduces yet another unexpected element: the familial. He describes the more experienced Panthers addressing younger people as patriarchs talking to their descendants, and this familial entity actually includes himself: indeed, of David Hilliard, a Black Panther with whom he spent much time in the United States, he writes; "For two months I was to be David's son. I had a black father thirty years younger than myself" (*PL*, 261).

From Invisible to Visible

Reflecting in *Prisoner of Love* upon the goals and strategies of the Black Panthers, Genet remarks:

> But the world can be changed by other means than the sort of wars in which people die: power may be at the end of a gun, but sometimes it is at the end of the shadow or image of a gun. (*PL*, 84)

Here, while not denying the efficacy of conventional revolutionary praxis (the gun), Genet suggests that a politics other than materialist (the image of a gun) might also be effective. As in his analysis of May '68, he recognizes the importance of a subversive aesthetic, therefore lending revolutionary efficacy to the realm of representation as well as to actions of a tangible order. Before exploring the tension between the two modes and their many articulations in Genet's texts about the Black Panthers, it is useful to outline, as a starting point, his views on race and racial oppression.

Though Genet did not formally theorize race any more than he did gender, he nonetheless offered a number of explicit or implicit comments on the subject, scattered in a variety of texts, such as his political articles, his introduction to George Jackson's prison letters and *Prisoner of Love*. And, of course, there's *The Blacks*. In the same way that Genet repeatedly claimed that if he joined the Panthers' struggle it is because they had requested his support (implying that to have taken the initiative himself would have been presumptuous), he never failed to point out that he wrote *The Blacks* because he had been asked to do so. Indeed, the play had been commissioned in the 1950s by the theater director Raymond Rouleau who very specifically wanted a work that could be performed by a group of Black franco-phone actors. Genet complied with the request, and *The Blacks* made its debut in Paris in 1959, directed by the already famous Roger Blin, and two years later in New York at the Saint Mark's Playhouse, di-rected by Gene Frankel, and with James Earl Jones, Maya Angelou and Cicely Tyson in the main roles. Both productions were highly successful. When asked about the play's political impact, Genet ex-pressed a position similar to the one he took in relation to *The Maids* and *The Screens:* one of skepticism, verging on disinterest. In a 1964 *Playboy* interview, he said: "If my plays help the Blacks, that's not my concern. I don't think they do anyway. I believe that action, a direct struggle against colonialism, does much more for Blacks than a play" (*ED*, 23). Elsewhere, foregrounding his later comment that *The Screens* was a play against France (rather than in favor of Algeria), he claimed that *The Blacks* was a play against Whites (rather than in favor of Blacks),[5] but he went no further than that.

Nonetheless, many Blacks recognized in Genet a valuable *porte pa-role.* James Baldwin, for one, was fascinated by *The Blacks* and at-tended many rehearsals in Paris.[6] Sarah Maldoror, a member of the African and Caribbean acting troupe that initially performed the play in France, affirmed at the time in an interview in *L'Express* that "Genet's play will help you understand us better. It's the only play that we've found at the moment at our disposal to educate you, to try to translate how ridiculous your idea of us is."[7] Another member of the troupe said of Genet: "He could have been black himself."[8] The play was shown in the United States at a time when Blacks were be-ginning to make up an important section of theater audiences in New York, White notes, and adds that "their laughter, their participa-tion, their pleasure during scenes expressing Black anger, contempt and desire for revenge startled the white audience."[9] These positive reactions notwithstanding, it is difficult to extract from the play any-thing that resembles a coherent political analysis of race relations: *The Blacks* is pervaded by masquerade and transvestism (Blacks play Whites, men play women) and the line between reality and perfor-mance is blurred (a mock trial takes place on stage while another, possibly authentic, takes place off stage). Yet, in contrast to this pow-erfully denaturalizing vision, when the two characters of Village and Virtue tell of their love for each other, they draw on an aesthetics of negritude with essentialist overtones—underlying the co-presence, here also, of the network of opposite forces that pervade much of Genet's work.

Ten years later, at the height of his involvement with the Panthers, Genet was interviewed in *Le Nouvel Observateur*. When asked if he'd have written *The Blacks* in the same way after knowing the Panthers, he flatly refused to talk about his past or future literary work. His only concern was to document for a French audience the intense racial oppression under which Black Americans lived. At this point, rather than in the vague colonial/postcolonial context of his play, Genet's analysis was grounded in the specific politics of the United States and developed within a framework of historical materialism. For example, in "Letter to American Intellectuals," a text based on a speech given at the University of Connecticut in March 1970, he explained: "The origin of racism is socio-economic. We must be very precisely conscious of this fact, for therein lies the point of departure of our solidarity with Blacks and the Black Panther Party" (*ED*, 45). Genet also often pointed out that, for Black Americans, history is short—going back only three to four hundred years—and that the starting point of both the oppression and rebellion, as well as of the political structures under which Blacks continue to live, is slavery. To reach beyond this point to an imaginary Africa is therefore not necessary to the struggle, Genet argued. Like the Panthers, Genet rejected cultural nationalism and did not believe that an investment in African identity and a celebration of African culture and heritage would do very much to bring about political freedom. In fact, to surround oneself with various cultural artifacts of a long lost past suggests an attempt to ignore rather than redress the reality of one's present situation in American society, Genet argued, and, furthermore, can be viewed by the oppressor as reassuring folklore (*ED*, 74–75). In addition, the Panthers' analysis of their situation as that of colonized subjects within the United States made sense to Genet. At the University of Connecticut he upheld this view and went even further, insisting that the Panthers' struggle inscribed itself in a class struggle. Positing a sympathetic left-wing audience, he explained: "By virtue of the fact that the Black Panthers and us, Whites, have the same enemy, the police, and beyond the police, the White administration, and beyond the White administration, high finance, we know that our struggle is a class struggle" (*ED*, 45). This point—that the Panthers' struggle transcended race, that it was of a global, socialist nature—is the one that Genet repeated the most. Since none of the official political parties were concerned with true equality for Black Americans, the only recourse was socialism; the struggle, then, was not only against racism but, rather, a global one that should be shared by all leftist people throughout the world, Genet insisted (*ED*, 57). Taking slavery as its starting point and the development of capitalism as its driving force, then, Genet's analysis of racial oppression in the United States was in many respects derived from conventional marxism.

In the *Nouvel Observateur* interview, Genet explained that it was to the Panthers' seriousness of purpose that he was first drawn and that he would not have supported them "if the Panthers had been nothing more than a gang of young Blacks playing havoc with the preserves of the Whites, thieves dreaming only—only!—of cars and women, bars and drugs" (*PL*, 259). This is a noteworthy critique from one who, some time back, celebrated thievery for thievery's sake and who took quite some pleasure in "playing havoc" with the preserves of the bourgeois; one in whom the fleeting glimpse through prison windows of a German warplane gave rise to lyrical expressions of delight. Not so now: in his analyses of racism in the United States Genet recognized a clear distinction between oppressor and oppressed and no longer found it thrilling to blur that line; and in the struggle for the freedom of one from the other, he valued organization and methods. Similar to his approval in May '68 of Cohn-Bendit's demands (that university cafeterias be open to workers, for example), Genet was also touched by the fact that the Panthers combined their revolutionary vision with grassroots practicality: they patrolled the streets and documented police violence; they taught "legal first aid" (everyone's basic rights when dealing with arrest or police brutality); they instituted breakfast programs and educational programs for children. Further, he applauded the fact that the Panthers' Ten Point Platform incorporated principles of marxist revolutionary praxis and hence provided a radical alternative to mainstream civil rights movements; he respected their use of arms, arguing that in the face of four hundred years of violence to preach nonviolence would be the height of hypocrisy: "To speak to [the Party] members about pacifism or non-violence would be a criminal act. For it would be to preach them an evangelical virtue no white man is capable of attaching to his own existence"* (*ED*, 51).

Genet was cognizant of the statistics that illustrated ongoing White violence and often recited them in detail to illustrate his arguments: twenty-four Panthers killed by the police between October 1968 and 1969; later, George Jackson killed, Angela Davis in jail, many more deaths, many more hideously unfair trials. In the May Day speech he delivered at Yale he expressed regret that there was no American intellectual to launch a *J'Accuse* in support of the Panthers and furthered the parallel with the Dreyfus Affair and antisemitism in France: "Previously, in France, there was a culprit: it was the Jew. Here, in the past and present, it is the Black"* (*ED*, 51). In this piece he expands his commentary on the process of automatic criminalization, explaining that the young Black man in jail is not assumed to be the son of a polite Black man who obeys the laws of Church and State but, rather, is inevitably imagined as the descendant of "one who three hundred years ago killed a White; took part in a mass runaway, robbing and pillaging and pursued by hounds; charmed and then raped a white woman, and was hanged without trial"* (*PL*, 48). It is an easy step to suggest a relationship here between the orphaned Genet falsely accused of being a thief (the scenario suggested by Sartre) and his understanding of the instant demonization and criminalization of Blacks, an understanding that serves, here, to justify an espousal of violence as legitimate self-defense.

However, as necessary to the Panthers' enterprise as the paramilitary, revolutionary or grassroots aspect of their struggle was their reliance on performance and images. Earlier, Genet had thought it was a mistake for students in May '68 to occupy a theater, the only place where theatricality does not conceal power. In *Prisoner of Love* he suggests that the reason for the lack of efficient political power in a theater is the predetermined nature of such a performance space: the well-defined acting area, the audience's awareness of the conventions involved, the actors' loss of spontaneity through rehearsals. In contrast to this he posits the very powerful nature of the theatricality relied upon by the Black Panthers in their revolutionary endeavors, powerful because its only locus was their body and on their performance no curtain ever fell. Indeed, Genet at length expressed his delight for the Panthers' very conscious self-representation: their paramilitary yet stylish and never drab way of dressing, the tension and poise in their manner of circulating in cities. Also theatrical was their seductive and inflamed manner of expression. The anger in the tone and timbre of their discourse was unsettling enough, Genet notes, and the hyperbolic mode fully justified for it was sustained by and conducive to action. Most crucial of all is the fact that this was a group of people who reacted to oppression not by hiding but by showing themselves off:

> The Black underwent a metamorphosis in himself. He had been invisible; he became visible. And this visibility was accomplished in various ways. Black is not a color in itself, but with a pigmentation showing every shade of density the Black can wear clothes that are veritable feasts of color. Against a black skin, light or dark, matching tones or contrasts of gold and azure, pink and mauve, are all equally striking. But the set cannot disguise the tragic scene being played before it. The eyes are alive and they give forth a terrifying eloquence. (*PL*, 84)

This metamorphosis from invisible to visible, this alternative to the White perception of a uniform mass of blackness, this reappropriation of bodies in individual diversity, bodies as base of harmonies, décor, backdrop, Genet elsewhere calls an illumination of existence. Against the décor, a drama is supported but not overshadowed by the Aaesthetics: "The eyes are alive and give forth a terrifying eloquence" (*PL*, 84). Whatever the individual variations to the backdrop, the drama of oppression and struggle from oppression that was being played out was common to all Blacks. This illumination, "by crackling, by sparkling, and finally by making not only visible but also luminous the Black question" (*PL*, 47), was successful, effected real change, for the Whites were affected by it. They saw the terrifying eloquence and they were terrified. Intent on preventing others from denying their existence, the Panthers made sure that White America was now confronted with the sight of them, and this was a spectacle it could neither assimilate nor respond to. The territory that the Panthers most successfully invaded was White consciousness:

> When the Panthers Afro haircut hit the whites in the eye, the ear, the nostril and the neck, even got under their tongues, they were panic-stricken. How could they defend themselves in the subway, in the bus, the office and the lift against all this vegetation, this springing, elastic growth like an extension of pubic hair? . . .Where could they have found insults fierce enough to smooth all those hairy sweaty, black faces, when every curly whisker on each black chin had been cherished and nurtured for dear life! (*PL*, 218)

An earlier chapter of this work explored how elements crucial to the aesthetic/political style known as camp operate in Genet's conception of gender. Similar elements are present in the way Genet views and represents the Panthers: indeed, one can very easily draw a connection between what he describes as the Panthers' emphasis on visual appearance, manner of dress, external style—all of which operate on their own body and tends towards the constitution of an identity both within the group and for the outside world—and Esther Newton's definition of camp as "life as theater." Again, this should not be taken to mean that there exists an "authentic" self that the performative role conceals. For the Panthers, "no curtain fell on the show," there was no retreat. Further, also common to camp, to Genet's conception of gender and to the Panthers' self-representation is the element of excess (one remembers, in Divine, the hyperbolic gesture, the overemphatic language and so on), as Genet writes: "Excess in display, in words, in attitude, swept the Panthers to ever greater excess" (*PL*, 85). Such an excess, both in drag and here, has a dual effect: first, it unfailingly captivates the gaze of others, commands attention if not a response; further, by producing an abundance that exceeds the terms of a strict, masculine, capitalist exchange economy, it challenges the very terms of that economy.

Yet the Panthers did not rely on theatricality alone, for also challenging the terms of that economy and acting as a counterpoint to the excess in appearance and attitude was the very sobering reality of the gun they prominently displayed, thereby avoiding the charge of carrying a concealed weapon. An immediately recognizable marker of defiance and power (phallic and otherwise), the gun no doubt partook in the willful spectacle of the Panthers' self-representation. At the same time, it operated on other significant levels. Politically, this bearing of arms underlined the fact that the law that authorized possession of a gun, though surely designed by Whites and for Whites, could also serve Blacks. Further, on a practical level, the very obvious display of a weapon avoided the charge of its concealed and thus illegal carrying. This attention to the co-presence and mutual dependence of the aesthetic and the practical pervades Genet's representation of the group. Insistently, he points out that their stylistic exploits, however pleasing in and of themselves, would have been of little value and politically unsustainable without the backing of the rational analyses that informed their political platform. Whatever self-indulgence might at times have been displayed in their theatrics was largely compensated for by their less-than-frivolous reliance on historical materialism and the unglamorous, even humble, efforts with which they sustained their breakfast programs, for example. And, while in their speeches the verbal excess suggested an unstrategic intemperance, the Panthers' reliance, for their campus visits, on this far from accessible and already mythical French intellectual pointed, on the contrary, to careful forethought. Last, as a powerful counterpoint to the Panthers' showy appearance, Genet often invokes the harsh reality of the large number of them in jail ("really in a real jail made of real stones and concrete and steel"), often in solitary confinement, invisible to the world.

On several occasions Genet wrote about the media's role in disseminating an awareness of the Panthers' metamorphosis; about how, with the morning paper or evening news, the spectacle of the Panthers entered homes all across America. He had, much earlier, written of a similar process. Indeed, in the opening pages of *Our Lady of the Flowers*, Genet describes how the photographs of vacant-eyed murderers cut from the tattered newspapers that reach his cell adorn its wall and serve as catalysts of desire and creativity. In particular, that of Weidman (a German, accused by the French in 1937 of killing six people and the object of much sensationalism in the press) is a particularly powerful figure in his imaginary. In fact, the novel begins with a reflection on the fear that the reproduction of this photograph in the press instilled in the right-thinking, law-abiding reader: "His handsome face, multiplied by the presses, swept down upon all of France, to the remotest out-of-the-way villages, in castles and cabins, revealing to the doleful bourgeois that their daily lives are grazed by enchanting murderers" (*OLF*, 51). Many decades after his reflections on Weidman's photographs in the tabloids of the time, Genet explains how the Panthers used ever more effective mass media to reach and send fear into the heartland of America. If they so deliberately put together a bold and provocative image, it was to draw the attention not only of those immediately around them but of the press in search of eye-catching sensationalism. Their photographs were propagated far beyond the urban enclaves where they were taken and reached, as did Weidman's, all strata of society ("castles and cabins") and the most remote places. White Americans whose contact with Blacks might have been minimal, if at all existent, were confronted with what Genet refers to as a stream of uninterrupted images, fascinating and deeply unsettling, from the Party's creation in October 1966 to the end of 1970.

However, while Genet admired the manner in which the Panthers used the media to their own advantage to propagate their image until White Americans were haunted by it, he also recognized that this process was not without its drawbacks. Because of their dehistoricized, decontextualized nature, these images representing isolated moments of the struggle failed to convey the history of oppression that led to such conflict. Further, since the interest these images generated was based mainly on their shock value and sensationalism, they did not create in the reader of *Life Magazine*, for example, a desire to find out more about the social conditions under which Black Americans lived. As Genet points out in "Angela and Her Brothers," an article written in support of Angela Davis while she was in hiding, the press, while presenting snippets of news and startling photographs, does not bother to explain the interplay of factors that prompted the conflict behind the images. If the photographs caught the readers' attention, it was because of their novelty—never before had Black men marched with guns on the Sacramento capitol. Yet, with an *ad nauseam* reproduction of these images, novelty might easily wear off, and with the loss of novelty the startling, threatening aspects of these representations would also lose their edge. Genet, then, recognized that ultimately the media controlled how the images would be used and could easily succeed in showing the Panthers partaking in a bizarre and mindless practice of violence, producing an entertaining and insignificant spectacle isolated from history, especially when it involved what he called the "iridescent fringe": the permeable barrier between the Panthers and the Whites, those who emulated the Panthers' appearance, their contestatory emblems, their discourse, but lacked their courage and devotion to the cause; those who copied the oppositional style but not the content, who were not governed by revolutionary discipline, but came out at night in purely carnivalesque fashion.

The risks, however, were counteracted by the fact that behind the images there was an inescapable reality: that of visibly armed Panthers willing to sacrifice their life for their struggle. The sensational photographs were backed up by the complete engagement of a group of people devoted unto death to their cause, with a seriousness of purpose sorely lacking, for example, in the pacifist hippies or the idealist students of May '68. Because of his aversion to patriotism in general and to its sentimental displays in particular, one such image was particularly pleasing to Genet. This photograph, in fact, drew not only national but international attention: the widely publicized picture of the two Black athletes who, at the 1968 Mexico Olympics, defied protocol while receiving their medals by raising their leather-gloved hand in a clenched-fist salute while the American anthem played. This gesture was potent and disruptive on a number of levels; first, because it occurred at a moment when these two Black Americans were given the full attention of their compatriots and perhaps even a brief moment of respect. Then, it appropriated the solemnity of a ritual that reinforced not only an individual's allegiance to a nation but the nation's primacy over the individual (signaled by the hoisting of the flag, the playing of the anthem and the expression of humility that most athletes find fitting to adopt at that time, and by the expression "America won the Gold"). The gesture appropriated these elements and transformed them into a moment expressive of antagonism between the two. It also shattered the comforting myth that sports and athleticism were areas that transcend racial divisions as well as the one that posited the Olympic Games as an event fraternal and apolitical above all. At the end of August 1970, in "Angela and Her Brothers," Genet describes the famous photograph of the athletes in the following terms: "The Panthers appeared in full glory in Mexico where, during the Olympic games, two Black medalists saluted, on the podium, with their clenched fist gloved in Black" (*ED*, 73). He then continues: "This is the image of them one must retain, *but one must add to it that of an extremely dangerous reality*" (*ED*, 73, my emphasis). Here again, this comment that the realm of pure representation must be backed up by that of the real echoes Genet's insistence that the Panthers' metamorphosis from invisible to visible was a consequence of a joint effect: that of their stylistic innovations, working in conjunction with their rational analyses, concrete grass-root efforts and armed struggle.

POETRY AND METAMORPHOSIS

In Sartre's reference to the interplay of opposites in Genet's work, he describes the relationship between them not as a fusion or balance but as an oscillation. Genet himself has recourse to this term in a footnote to *The Thief's Journal*. In the opening page of this early work he writes of the close relationship between flowers and convicts, adding: "The fragility and delicacy of the latter are of the same nature as the brutal insensitivity of the latter" (*TJ*, 7). This sentence is footnoted with the following explanation: "My excitement is the oscillation from one to another" (*TJ*, 7). This term "oscillation" accurately describes how Genet, at different times, privileged one aspect or another of the Panthers' enterprise. While he made very clear the crucial importance of each, and the fact that they mutually sustained each other, he at times expressed intense enthusiasm for the practical and material side of the struggle, while he, in other instances, exalted the stylistic endeavors above all. On those occasions where the aesthetics of the revolt were privileged, it is clear that Genet found these not only a powerful intervention in the social realm, but personally pleasing to him also. On occasion, he went so far as to detect in their struggle a poetic element that closely coincides with those in his own work.

Reflecting in *Prisoner of Love* on the overall achievements of the Black Panthers, Genet observes: "So the Panthers were heading for either madness, metamorphosis of the Black community, death or prison. All these options happened, but the metamorphosis was by far the most important, *and that is why the Panthers can be said to have overcome through poetry*" (*PL*, 86, my emphasis). The link suggested here between the Panthers' metamorphosis (from invisible to visible) and poetry recalls an instance in *The Thief's Journal*, where, referring to his efforts to rehabilitate through writing a particularly somber period of his life, he wrote: "My victory is verbal and I owe it to the richness of the terms" (*TJ*, 36). It also recalls a memorable passage from another early work, *Our Lady of the Flowers*, in which Genet traces his own understanding of the poetic:

> Poetry is a vision of the world obtained by an effort, sometimes exhausting, of the taut, buttressed will. Poetry is willful. It is not an abandonment, a free and gratuitous entry by the senses; it is not to be confused with sensuality, but rather, opposing it, was born, for example, on Saturdays, when, to clean the rooms, housewives put the red velvet chairs, gilded mirrors, and mahogany tables outside, in the nearby meadows. (*OLF*, 226)

The passage begins with an opposition between abandonment and sensuality, two terms that do not produce poetry, and a tense effort of the will, which does, and which, in the context of *Our Lady of the Flowers*, is reminiscent of Divine's efforts at self-creation. In fact, these sentences are preceded by remarks against nature: "Hateful nature, antipoetic, ogress, swallowing up all spirituality" (*OLF*, 225). In the context of the Black Panthers, this distinction between abandonment and sensuality on the one hand, and a tense effort of the will on the other, parallels one referred to earlier, the one Genet made between them and the hippies, as he criticized the latters' formlessness, self-indulgence, and uncontrollable descent into drugs and praised the strict, tense, organized, strategic Black Panther Party. The image with which the quote ends—the house with its furniture sitting in a nearby meadow—connotes two things. First, a planned rearrangement of the customary order of existence, and second, a visible exposition, on the outside, of what customarily resides inside. This certainly echoes what was discussed in earlier chapters as a performative gender construction that challenges the existence of an inner core; it also relates to what is of concern here, the Panthers' metamorphosis from invisible (hidden) to visible (exhibited). The next passage, also from *Our Lady of the Flowers*, offers a further reflection on the subject:

> Quite some time before, the appearance on the village road of a bride wearing a black dress, though wrapped in a veil of white tulle, lovely and sparkling, like a young shepherd beneath the hoar frost, like a powdered blond miller or like Our Lady of the Flowers whom he will meet later on and whom I saw with my own eyes here in my cell one morning, near the latrines—his sleepy face pink and bristly beneath the soapsuds, which blurred his vision—revealed to Culafroy that poetry is something other than a melody of curves on sweetness, for the tulle snapped apart in abrupt, clear, rigorous icy facets. It was a warning. (*OLF*, 62)

The initial image again inverts customary expectations: obviously, the bride wearing black, and, further, the effect of the white tulle, which, rather than softening contours and creating a halo, does the contrary: "snapped apart into abrupt, clear, rigorous icy facets" (*OLF*, 62). There is, also, the bringing together of opposites: the white tulle over the black dress, the bride compared to men (the shepherd, the miller, Our Lady). And, as in the previous quote, Genet offers the admonition that poetry is "something other than a melody of curves on sweetness" (*OLF*, 62); further, the adjectives he uses to describe the tulle—abrupt, clear, rigorous—often appear in his descriptions of the Panthers. Also recurrent in these descriptions are motifs involving a conjunction of opposites, and describing, as is often the case in his novels of the 1940s (with the motif of the veiled phallus, for instance), differences of textures: the mix of the fluidity of certain brightly colored fabrics with the heaviness, solidity, substantial weightiness of the paramilitary leather jackets, boots and guns. As discussed earlier, Genet also insisted on the powerful effect of certain images reproduced in the media, such as the picture of visibly armed Panthers marching onto the state capitol or of the Black athletes responding to the star-spangled banner with a clenched-fist salute. These images certainly challenge the horizon of expectations of middle (White) America. In the first instance, as unexpected as a bride wearing black, is the leather glove raised against a backdrop of patriotic emblems. In the other instance, the image of visibly armed Panthers entering the California state capitol brought together law and order (the capitol) and its potential disruption. Black Panther Bobby Seale recalls its effect:

> And then as we began to walk, I noticed one thing. [White people] moved and stepped aside, and I saw some with their mouths hanging open, just looking, and they were saying with their eyes and faces and their expressions "Who the hell are these niggers with guns?" and some were just saying "Niggers with guns, niggers with guns," and I pointed them out as the enemy because they were confused.[10]

If these images appeared so powerful to Genet it is certainly because of the undeniable effect they had on an unprepared audience—confused the audience, as Seale notes— but, one might also add, because they relied upon an aesthetic that correlated with his own. They bring together opposite terms in a manner true to his own reflections on poetry in *Our Lady of the Flowers* and consistent with imagery that pervades his own work.

Admittedly, to assign a politically subversive value to the creation of such images that shatter conventional expectations and allow a glimpse of a new order is not original. In fact, in its literary form, this belief informed a French modernist tradition traceable from Rimbaud (*Il faut trouver une langue* [one must find a language]) to the surrealists and beyond. Yet, if Genet at times appears to privilege the poetic element in the Panthers' struggle, he never suggests that poetry in and of itself might usefully intervene in the social realm. In fact, in the Fichte interview, he unambiguously states that he does not believe that revolutions in the literary realm can in any way change the order of the world, or even the vision one might have of it. They might render one's vision sharper, more subtle, more complex, but they will not affect a significant transformation. The power of the Panthers' poetics is that they were performed on their very bodies—bodies involved in an armed stuggle, encountering the daily risk of jail or death.

Literature and Revolution

While Genet must have been aware that the support he brought the Panthers was enabled by his literary fame, in their presence he refused to answer questions about himself and his work. In fact, he expressed irritation at such queries and often deflated the importance of his past achievements. In a brief statement preceding a debate organized by the Panthers at MIT he began by warning the audience that he would find it indecent to talk about himself while Bobby Seale was awaiting trial and asserted his complete commitment to the Panther's cause, which, he made it understood, belonged to a realm quite separate from and much more important than that of his artistic endeavors. Sometime later, in a 1973 interview published in the *Journal of Palestine Studies*, he drew a theoretical distinction between politics and literature: "I firmly believe that the work of the artist should be left free" and in the Fichte interview of 1976, he made a pragmatic distinction between the artist and the revolutionary: "In revolutionary action, you put your body on the line. In the work of art, you perhaps put your reputation on the line but your body is not in danger" (*ED*, 147).

Not only did he dissociate himself from his past work and literary persona, but in the speeches delivered in the Panthers' presence from March to July 1970 Genet eschewed literariness and maintained a narrow and very clear focus. Though, of course, his mode of expression was elegant and forceful (qualities impossible for Genet to avoid), the style was either primarily informational (when he offered statistics regarding police violence, for instance), analytical (when he developed his views on racism) or rhetorical (in his calls for action). In the speech delivered at Yale on 1 May 1970 he apologized for the fact that his habits tended to be those of a vagabond rather than a revolutionary and guarded against the intrusion of a poetic register in his statements: "I mean that no unreality should creep into my own statements for it would be prejudicial to the Black Panther Party and to Bobby Seale who is really in a real jail made of stones and concrete and steel"* (*ED*, 46). Here he clearly makes a distinction between politics and the real (the materiality of stone and steel) on the one hand and irreality and the poetic on the other. However, a change gradually took place, and Genet's speeches and writings on the Panthers moved away from objective analysis to increasingly literary elements.

What occurs in this second group of texts, written between July 1970 and March 1971, is precisely what Genet avoided in his May Day speech: the creeping of unreality into his statements. Rather than resisting flights away from the customary factual information and analyses, the writing takes off on tangents into a realm where imagination, myth and poetry reign. In "The Assassination of George Jackson," designed as a preface to a brochure edited by Michel Foucault's *Groupe d'Information sur les Prisons* [Group of Information on Prisons], literariness dominates and a very new understanding of the function of the writer vis-à-vis revolutionaries is put forward:

> I think that one must not refuse revolutionaries, when it becomes necessary to them, this sort of magnificence of reverie and act, above all when the act must become exemplary, that is, when it serves to show, brilliantly, the meaning and direction of a life that has striven to be a thorough struggle against false fatalism.* (*ED*, 116)

Assuming that the "one" represents a writer in general (and Genet in particular), the sentence constitutes an authorization, even an advocation, for him to depict the revolutionary in a manner unrestricted by the laws of realism. Indeed, "magnificence of reverie and act" suggests a representation that allows for grandeur, splendor and fantasy. This literary representation and possible transformation (at least, aggrandizement) of the act is not gratuitous but has a precise function, a function that goes beyond the text: it helps the act become "exemplary," Genet explains. This is an odd term for him to use, one that is not recurrent in his discourse, but passages from *Prisoner of Love* clarify the meaning he has in mind. There, he writes about exemplary images as those that one might wish to project during one's life to constitute one's specificity and that might remain after one's death to create "an unforceful radiance at once sweet and strong" (*PL,* 261). He explains that an image might be exemplary not because it is designed to set an example but "in the special and paradoxical sense that it is unique" (*PL,* 261). Though each is separate and unique, such images join together to make up memory and history: "From Greece to the Panthers, history has been made out of man's need to detach and project fabulous images, to send them as delegates into the future, to act in the very long term, after death" (*PL,* 262). Clearly, then, for Genet in this instance, history is constituted not by factual, documentary accounts but, rather, by something on the order of Greek epics, myths, medieval chansons—and quite different from the understanding he relied upon when advocating marxist-derived analyses of Black oppression.

Also noteworthy in the quote from "The Assassination of George Jackson" is the reference to the life of revolutionaries as a "thorough struggle against false fatalism" (*ED,* 116). Here, Genet is no doubt referring to the paralyzing belief—uniformly and simplistically essentialist—that race and class hierarchies as well as the oppressive structures that ensue, are predetermined, unavoidable, natural. Detectable here is a passing reference to earlier concerns, for false fatalism can include the fallacious belief in a predetermined gender. One remembers Divine's self-creation: the creation, out of a block of marble, of her feminine self; and one might venture that this refusal to fulfill societal expectations of immobility, this revolt against falsely naturalized and impermeable categories, is one thing that drag queens and revolutionaries have in common. Further along in the article, Genet explains that the struggle against false fatalism includes what he calls the "amazing" action of Jonathan Jackson: the "truly heroic attempt to rescue three black comrades at the San Rafael courthouse, on August 7, 1970"* (*ED,* 116).[11] Other such acts that Genet refers to in the same piece are George Jackson's relentless political education while behind bars and his joining the Black Panther Party while serving his sentence. Such acts are what led him to be (unofficially) considered a political prisoner, resulting in the perpetual renewal of his sentence, and, ultimately, his death only a few days before he planned to make what probably might have been his last court appearance. From such amazing actions a *rêverie* ensues, one Genet relates in an article he wrote immediately following George Jackson's assassination in August 1971:

A few hours after Jackson's death, I had this dream, half awake: nine months, or a little more, apart, Jonathan and George violently exited the prison, womb of stone, amidst streams of blood. This expulsion resembled the birth of two twins of the same age. It was not their mother who had given birth to them that night, for she was there, impassable but present, she watched. If this was a new birth, into life as well as into death, who was giving birth, if not History, to two black men covered in blood as in all births?* (*ED*, 108)

Genet then goes on to warn that such images—the rebirth of George and Jonathan Jackson as Black Gemini—operate within a new Black mythology that must perform a concrete work of erosion against the "scintillating mythology" of the White world. Images of rebirth are pervasive in the two texts that follow Jackson's death. On a practical level, Genet insists that this death is not in vain: those young Blacks killed daily at the hands of the police will survive "among peoples oppressed by the white world, thanks to the resounding voice of George Jackson"* (*ED*, 111). On other occasions, *rêverie* takes over and the motif is cloaked in a religious, resurrection-like quality:

George Jackson rises again, brushes himself off, now illustrious, that is to say luminous, and bearing a light so bright that it designates him and all Black Americans.* (*ED*, 111)

This move away from factual considerations and towards an inclusion of the literary occurs in all of the pieces that Genet wrote at the time in support of George Jackson. In "For George Jackson," a text formed of fragments and which was to serve as a manifesto signed by French artists and intellectuals in favor of Jackson's release, Genet avoids considerations on Black oppression of an historical or documentary nature. He also leaves behind the patient, almost pedagogical tone of his earlier interventions. Perhaps because he wrote this piece from the vantage point of the Middle East where he had begun his travels with the Palestinians, Genet now fuses together, with a sweeping gesture, postcolonial Europe and White America and refers to it as (a much maligned) "Christian Occident." Intent on drawing attention to Jackson's trial, the text is a virulent call to action, emotional in tone and metaphorical in style, addressed to a *vous:* an apathetic White audience, glued to its chairs, full of "evangelical love, cinghalese tea and whisky." Genet's denunciation of the prison system is not at all analytically developed in this piece, but is alluded to in the contrast he draws between a dreamlike "pink and blue California" and the brutal gas chambers of its state prisons. A recurrent motif of this piece is the vertiginous abyss that separates Blacks from Whites, an abyss symbolized by Jackson's trial, which "has been going on for the last 300 years." In a contemporaneous essay, "The Red and the Black," the literary—Stendhalian—reference is obvious in the title. There are other connotations which Genet underlines in the body of the text:

> These men and this woman of whom I speak [George and Jonathan Jackson, and Angela Davis] are Black but that is not their most inexpiable crime. Black without any doubt but also red and the optical nerve of blond Americans becomes frenzied, does not know what image or what color to seize.* (*ED*, 103)

At the core of this piece is the argument that George Jackson is innocent, that he could not have killed the prison guard, but the arguments do not rely on evidence or analysis. Rather, they draw on metaphor. Genet first posits that Jackson's writing in and of itself constitutes a murder: a murder accomplished in the solitude of jail against White America, against America's will to power. To write this text, which demanded such vision and psychic energy, is an act simply irreconcilable with a much more petty and simple assassination of a prison guard: it is impossible that Jackson committed both.

Clearly, then, there is a striking difference in style between Genet's initial set of texts on the Panthers and those that he wrote after leaving the United States (from the summer of 1970 onwards). Several factors no doubt account for the evolution. First, the circumstances of their creation are not comparable: the first group was designed to be delivered as brief speeches on university campuses at a time when Genet was living and traveling with the Panthers. During this period, he was quite dissociated from France and the literary world. The second set of texts, written in more familiar surroundings after he left the United States, were for the most part intended to remain in written form. The most crucial factor, however, in Genet's return to literariness was his encounter with George Jackson's *Soledad Brother* in July 1970. The preface that Genet wrote for this work might be the most widely read of his political pieces, for in the United States alone this book sold more than half a million copies during its first year. The prestigious press Gallimard published the French edition in May 1971, and, shortly after that, the preface was published in the most reputable, widely read and fairly conservative newspaper, *Le Monde*.

An immediately notable aspect of Genet's preface to *Soledad Brother* is that, as was "For George Jackson," it is written in fragments (a literary rather than journalistic or oratorical form). Another is that Genet gives equal weight to political and artistic issues, whereas up to that point he had insistently made a distinction between writers and revolutionaries. For instance, when the French journalist Michèle Manceaux asked him in an interview in the 1970s whether he still intended to produce literature, Genet avoided a direct answer and commented that Brecht had done nothing for communism and that the French revolution had not been provoked by Beaumarchais' *The Marriage of Figaro*. However, in this preface, not only are revolutionaries valorized (as they are in all of his recent writings), but the notion of an "authentic writer" is praised also, and George Jackson is declared to be both—to excel in the realm of both action and representation. Earlier, in his May Day speech, Genet had declared that precisely because Bobby Seale was in jail ("a real jail of stone and steel") no unreality should creep into the statements of support for Jackson that he was about to make. Here (where the prisoner is also the speaking subject), he offers a very different view of the effects of incarceration on language: he says that, in Jackson's writing, he recognizes the unmistakable stamp of literature created in jail. There are parallels between Jackson's text and those of Sade or Artaud, whose writing is characterized by audacity, vision and correctness of ideas (and in whose statements plenty of unreality crept). Further, Genet implies, these prison letters bear common elements with his own work. One of these is a shared relationship towards official, correct language. Genet talks about the dilemma encountered by Black Americans regarding their use of White English and recognizes the fact that there is no solution for the writer who wants to be understood but to adopt the language of the enemy, but that he can, and should, modify it slightly: "To accept it in all its richness, to augment its richness" (*ED*, 186). To resort to the official language while operating a subtle transformation is a process that Genet himself claims he adopted in his own literary production: because he wanted those whom he called his torturers to understand him, he used a classical French, displaced somewhat in the direction of sumptuousness.

Certainly, this preface is not without its trenchant political analysis, its caustic reflections on the judicial system and the exacerbated racism of jails. Yet one senses Genet's delight at this new immersion into the literary, with this forceful work that brings together vastly divergent elements, for, he explains, it is at the same time a personal testimony that reflects the development of its author and a document of social and historical value that transcends an individual trajectory. Jackson's letters, though written without literary intent, when brought together form an undeniably literary work for which Genet's praise is limitless, especially because as well as being a poem of love and struggle this work is a manifesto and a call to revolt; and because its author is both a poet and a prisoner awaiting the death penalty. Such conjunctions of opposites, which to Sartre would have seemed politically useless, aesthetically gratuitous and generally irritating, to Genet are irresistible.

4

Bullets at the Milky Way

In one of Shakespeare's tragedies, the archers loose their arrows
against the sky, and I wouldn't be surprised if some of the
fedayeen, feet firmly on the ground but angered at so much
beauty arching out of the land of Israel, had taken aim and
fired their bullets at the Milky Way.
—*Prisoner of Love,* 7

EUROPE ERASED

IN AN ARTICLE ON JEAN GENET'S LATE WORKS, EDWARD SAID JUDGES
the aging writer's commitment to the Palestinian resistance to be the
most dangerous political choice and the scariest journey of all, because "only Palestine has not been co-opted in the West by either the
dominant liberal or the dominant establishment political culture."[1]
Undoubtedly, Genet was aware of the boldness of his choice, and the
radical nature of his support for the Palestinians (which immediately
followed his involvement with the Black Panthers and lasted until his
death) made it all the more seductive. As had his work with the Black
Panthers, this new surge of political activity surprised more than one.
Yet Genet was no stranger to the Middle East.

Indeed, following his internment at the boys' penitentiary at Mettray, Genet enlisted in the French military, and, to escape what he already found to be an unbearably stifling "atmosphère française" and
discover what he foresaw as a different world, he volunteered to serve
abroad (*ED*, 300). At the age of eighteen, then, he was sent to Syria
(which was held under French mandate from 1920 to 1940). Talking
to Hubert Fichte much later, Genet fondly remembers the happy
times he had there and reveals that his concerns had little to do with

the proper maintenance of French rule (*ED*, 172). He recalls that he was in love with a sixteen-year-old hairdresser in Damascus and that he felt very much at ease with him, his family, and the entire city. The French military was under strict orders to be armed at all times, to circulate in groups of three and to never give way on the narrow sidewalks to Arabs, be they women or old men. Genet proudly announces that he broke these rules, happily wandered alone in the marvelous *souks* of the city, and always treated its inhabitants with utmost politeness and respect.

In another interview, with TV personality Bertrand Poirot-Delpech, he makes it clear that his refusal to obey the French code of conduct in the colonies was motivated not only by chivalry but by a definite feeling of empathy with the colonized: "I felt completely on the side of the Syrians" (*ED*, 228). While it was not at the time politically formulated, this initial feeling of empathy did develop later into a coherent anticolonialist stance and then into a clearly pro-Palestinian one. Interestingly, Said considers Genet's attraction to the Arab world in general and to the Palestinians in particular to be free of politically suspect attitudes. There are certainly enough precedents of excursions into North Africa by sexually motivated Europeans, whether accompanied by literary pretenses or not, to justify the question: "Does his love for the Palestinians nevertheless amount to a kind of overturned or exploded Orientalism? Or is it a sort of reformulated colonialist love of handsomely dark men?"[2] Said however goes on to argue against this possibility and explains:

> However he might have made his initial contact with the Arabs (*Un Captif* suggests that he first fell in love with an Arab while an eighteen-year-old soldier stationed in Damascus half a century ago), he entered the Arab space and lived in it not as an investigator of exoticism but as someone for whom the Arabs had actuality and a presence that he enjoyed, felt comfortable with, even though he was, and remained, different. In the context of a dominant Orientalism that commanded, codified, articulated virtually all Western knowledge and experience of the Arab/Islamic world, there is something quietly but heroically subversive about Genet's extraordinary relationship with the Arabs.[3]

To reach this conclusion, Said relies on his direct experience with Genet, on that of close friends they shared, and also on his reading of *The Screens* and *Prisoner of Love*. Of these, he writes: "Both were written in a frankly partisan mode . . . *The Screens* in support of Algerian resistance during the height of the colonial struggle, *Prisoner of Love* in support of the Palestinian resistance from the late '60s until his death in 1986 . . . so that one is left in no doubt where Genet stood."[4] In fact, Said considers those works to be pervaded by a revolutionary energy both dislocating and rigorous as well as efficient.

Ironically, personal empathy and subversive energy notwithstanding, Genet's first contact with the Palestinians occurred through French academic channels: Phillipe Sollers and other members of the *Tel Quel* group introduced him in 1969 to the Palestinian representative in Paris. Further drawing his attention to the struggle were the violent events of Black September a year later—events that, interestingly, did not pit the Palestinians against the Israelis but against the Jordanians. Jordan was the place to which many Palestinians had fled after the founding of Israel and in even greater numbers following the annexation of Gaza and the West Bank in 1967. Conflicts between them and King Hussein intensified to the point that, yielding to U.S. pressure, the latter signed a cease-fire with Israel and designated the Palestinians as enemies. Hussein withdrew his troops from the Israeli-Jordanian border and deployed them in and around Amman—a Palestinian stronghold. The result was a civil war that killed many thousands of Palestinians. It was when Genet heard of the bloodshed that he felt compelled to lend his support to their struggle, yet he describes this moment of recognition as one involving aesthetic judgment more than coherent analysis: "I had greeted the revolt as a musical ear recognizes a right note" (*PL*, 16).

After the recognition that the plight of the Palestinians had touched him, and profoundly, Genet once again displayed the full extent of his *disponibilité* [availability]: that very September he immediately accepted an invitation to visit refugee camps and military bases and, as when he illegally entered the United States through Canada, was delighted to further defy authorities by flying to Lebanon and then being smuggled to Jordan by car. Originally, he had intended to stay for only one week, but this initial encounter with the Palestinians was a powerful one and he remained in the Middle East for eight months. This visit yielded many of the experiences recounted later, in fragmented form, in *Prisoner of Love*, as well as in his first text on the Palestinians: a commentary on a series of photographs of the camps published by the photo-journal *Zoom Magazine*. One of its themes is familiar: as he had often done in his writings on the Black

Panthers, Genet again invokes his memories of May '68 in Paris, the event that caught his attention initially for aesthetic reasons but in which he saw strong yet unfulfilled political potential and a reliving of which he often and nostalgically yearned for. The student revolt and Palestinian struggle share an aesthetic, but the Palestinians have the very definite advantage of being armed. He explains:

> What was happening in the wooded mountains of Jerash looked a little like May '68 in Paris, with the important difference that the fedayeen were armed. As in Paris, on certain days, on the bases or on the roads or trails linking the bases, there was a breeziness close to effusion.* (*ED*, 92)

Once again, then, Genet encounters the irresistible combination with which the Panthers so completely seduced him: a struggle that has a festive, slightly unreal air—elsewhere in the text he calls it "a light-hearted fête, dreamlike"(*ED*, 92) as well as a very tangible, material combat.

Genet returned to the Middle East for a month and a half at the end of September 1971 and again for four months in 1972. In November of that year he set out on his fourth journey but soon noticed he was under Jordanian surveillance; realizing the risks he and his Palestinian friends were taking, he left within a few days only to return a decade later during the Lebanese war. On that occasion, he arrived shortly after the murder of the recently elected president of Lebanon (Bashir Gemayel of the Christian Right) when Israeli forces entered Beirut and encircled the Palestinian refugee camps of Sabra and Shatila. This did not stop the right-wing Christian phalangists from invading the camps and torturing and killing close to a thousand Palestinians during the night of 16 September. Genet was one of the very few Europeans to witness the shocking aftermath of the massacre: two days after it took place he found a way to enter the camps and observe the extent of the violence and destruction. He returned to Paris a few days later and recorded his passionate outrage in "Four Hours at Shatila," sparing no detail in his minute descriptions of the mutilated corpses that lined the streets. The following summer, in Morocco, he began writing *Prisoner of Love* and made only one further journey to the Middle East: a last pilgrimage, in July 1984, in search of the people and sites that had become dear to him. He handed the manuscript to Gallimard six months before his death.

Of all of Genet's works, his last escapes definition and reduction the most. Though there are a number of recurring characters and themes, the narrative lines of *Prisoner of Love* are meandering and profusely digressive. Fragmented recollections of time spent in Palestinian camps and military bases give way to reflections on music, love, history, politics or death. Factual, empirical analyses mingle with the most lyrical imagery. The book is divided into two sections, called "Souvenirs 1" and "Souvenirs 2," hence conferring to the text a status close to that of a memoir. Indeed, much of the text was written several years after the events it describes, and Genet is not without recognizing the distortions due to the fallibility of memory. Further, he also recognizes that objectivity was never a goal and that the very structure of the narrative guarantees the highly subjective nature of his account:

> But I must stress that it is my eyes that saw what I thought I was describing, and my ears that heard it. The form I adopted from the beginning for this account was never designed to tell the reader what the Palestinian revolution was really like. . . . The construction, organization and layout of the book, without deliberately intending to betray the facts, manage the narrative in such a way that I probably seem to be a privileged witness or even a manipulator. . . . All these words to say: this is my Palestinian revolution, told in my own chosen order. As well as mine there is the other, probably many others. (*PL*, 308)

Genet, then, is well aware that any literary representation (or, in fact, any linguistic representation) of an event modifies it somewhat. Discourse is never transparent even in the best-intentioned attempt at objectivity, but there is probably more at play when he says "this is my Palestinian Revolution." It was his because he chose to interpret it and experience it in a certain way, to freely exercise his poetic license, and to very deliberately rearrange events and memories according to the configuration of his choice. It was his also because it performed a very powerful function in his imaginary: his travels in the Middle East and the time he spent with the Palestinians enabled him to construct what he calls his own "space of liberty." Indeed, in the last pages of *Prisoner of Love*, he explains that just as an artist dissatisfied with a drawing can, with a few strokes of an eraser, make it completely disappear and have in front of him a perfectly white sheet of paper again, his representation of Palestine was preceded by a complete erasure of Europe. That blank space had become a "space of liberty" ready to be filled with his own experience and representation of the Palestinian resistance. Already when as a teenager Genet felt suffocated by France and requested to be posted overseas, he perceived Syria as a freer, utopian space. Quite different from the United States which was completely alien and generally repulsive to him and where his sympathies belonged to one specific group only, he always felt at home in the Middle East. (In Said's words, "The Arabs had an actuality and a presence he enjoyed, felt comfortable with."[5]) In fact, Genet chose to spend his final years in Morocco and to be buried there. This does not mean, of course, that he was unaware of the oppressive political régimes that flourished in the region, for he often harshly criticized the policies of King Hussein of Jordan and the corrupted capitalism of Saudi Arabia and various emirates. Not surprisingly, though, what truly captured his passion is what he perceived as a revolutionary struggle that combined the aesthetics and politics that he cherished.

DISPLACEMENT AND DISSEMINATION

During a long-distance plane flight, Genet reflects upon the hardships that displacement and landlessness bring, his observations sparked by the actual sight of Palestinian refugee camps below or by photographs in the travel magazines that are often provided by the airlines:

> The fact that the tents were of many colors, because of the patches, made them pleasing to look at, especially to a western observer. If they looked at them from far enough away and on a misty day, people thought the camps must be happy places because of the way the colors of the patches seemed to match: those who lived beneath such harmony must be happy, or they wouldn't have taken the trouble to make the camps such a joy to the eye. (*PL*, 11)

This passage addresses an illusion most likely produced by an occidental gaze prone to initially interpret the colorful patchwork as an instance of whimsical and cheerful exotica rather than perceive that, in reality, the mottled effect is a consequence of the deterioration and lack of suitable means of repair of the tents. Because of a hazy atmosphere, or perhaps simply because of the distance from which they are perceived, the edges of the patches appear blurred, the discordant colors muted and an impression of harmony is created that heightens the pleasing effect. This appearance of harmony suggests to the Westerner that there is a willful intention behind what is really a haphazard assemblage of fabrics, an aesthetic intention which reflects the joy of the inhabitants inside the camps. Some pages later, Genet returns to the image of multicolored tents and to the illusion of peace and happiness they might project from afar to denounce the political reality that led to their existence: the expulsion of unwanted populations by imperialist powers. He does so in very material terms (refuse of settled nations, liquid waste, discharge) that underline the denial of the Palestinians' humanity:

> Whole nations don't become nomads by choice or because they can't keep still. We see them through the windows of airplanes or as we leaf through glossy magazines. The shiny pictures lend the camps an air of peace that diffuses itself through the whole cabin, whereas really they are just the discarded refuse of "settled" nations. These, not knowing how to get rid of their "liquid waste" discharge it into a valley or on to a hillside, preferably somewhere between the tropics and the equator. (*PL*, 12)

Later, Genet further denounces this illusion, drawing on and sustaining a type of inside/outside, appearance/reality opposition that, elsewhere, he more often than not undoes:

> We oughtn't to have let their ornamental appearance persuade us the tents were happy places. We shouldn't be taken in by sunny photographs. A gust of wind blew the canvas, the zinc and the corrugated iron away, and I saw the misery plain. (*PL*, 12)

Here, the core of pain beneath the cheerful shell is uncovered and this moment of unveiling is not unlike another in *Our Lady of the Flowers* where drag queens at a trial are called by their official (male) names rather than the sumptuous ones they had chosen for their feminine selves:

> Thus, in the eyes of our bewildered Lady, the little faggots from Pigalle to Place Blanche lost their loveliest adornment, their names lost their corolla, like the paper flowers that the dancer holds at his fingertips and which, when the ballet is over, is a mere wire stem. They were no longer the grove of crinkly paper that flowered on the terrace of cafés. They were misery in motley. (*OLF*, 281)

These passages clearly suggest that when addressing the politics and aesthetics of fragmentation and dispersal in *Prisoner of Love*, one should keep in mind that Genet was quite aware of the daily material reality of a displaced refugee population, as well as of the dangers of a superficial poeticization of the displacement. It is a fact easily overlooked, however, for while Genet was keenly aware of the cruel and profoundly dehumanizing consequences of diaspora and landlessness, he was also repelled by any form of nationalism; the co-existence of these two positions gives rise to some of the paradoxes that surface in his celebration of the Palestinian resistance. His profound distaste for nationalism is certainly what caused him to often repeat that the fedayeen were not fighting for a piece of land, that material goals were not at the forefront of their concerns. For example, he describes the struggle as "a movement that wishes itself to be very profound, much removed from a simple recovery of territories" (*PL*, 271, *mod*), not aiming for the establishment of a settled, internationally recognized, fully functional state with all its conventional appendages:

> The idea of accepting some territory, however small, where the Palestinians would have a government, a capital, mosques, churches, cemeteries, town halls, war memorials, racecourses and airfields where soldiers would present arms twice a day to foreign heads of state—the idea was such heresy that even to entertain it as a hypothesis was a mortal sin, a betrayal of the revolution. (*PL*, 266)

Genet goes on to say that the fedayeen's passions were aroused by the dynamic process of revolution and that what they were really seeking was "a great firework display of a revolution, a conflagration leaping from bank to bank, opera house to opera house, prison to law court, sparing only the oil wells" (*PL*, 266). In a 1983 interview published in the *Revue d'études Palestiniennes* he claims that he himself would not support them otherwise, that the day when the Palestinians would become a nation like any other nation he would no longer be at their side (*ED*, 282). These remarks recall a statement that Genet made to Hubert Fichte about Cuba, claiming that he had lost all interest in the place once the early revolutionary fervor had settled into all the conventional appendages of nationhood—a flag, a national anthem (*ED*, 154). When Genet reflects on what the Palestinians were fighting for, he does recognize the legitimate demands of a landless people but also discerns a more profound and less materially driven revolutionary energy. In the following passage he addresses the issue further:

> I got used to the fedayeen, sure that they thirsted for justice and wanted a fairer life, as they still said. These reasons for rebellion still existed, but underneath them . . . imperatives included a love of fighting and physical confrontation, together with an underlying desire for self-sacrifice, for glorious death if victory was impossible. (*PL*, 272, *mod*)

Once again, Genet invokes both substance and style, acknowledging the existence of conventional and tangible revolutionary goals—justice, equality—while perceiving more intriguing revolutionary motives, motives that are not part of theoretical revolutionary strategy. These other reasons have less to do with necessity than with desire: the carnal pleasure of the fight, the longing for a glorious, heroic death. The longing for a heroic death may well be what Genet obliquely refers to with the terms "vertigo" and "shadow" when he quotes a fedayee making a startling distinction between political and revolutionary engagement: "When someone makes a political choice, he ought to be quite clear; but when making a revolutionary choice, or entering a revolutionary vertigo, it is a shadier process" (*PL*, 296, *mod*).

The passage describing the aerial views of the refugee camps registers their transient, makeshift nature (the haphazard assembly of cloths), as the Palestinians created a home base wherever they could and moved again according to political circumstance. Genet clearly recognizes the oppressive nature of such uprootedness when it is enforced from the outside. Quite different is such mobility when freely chosen; it is then to be prized. For instance, in Genet's self-presentation, in the public persona that he carved for himself, there is always much emphasis on the fact that he had no fixed address (his passport showed that of his publisher) and that, when not incarcerated, he was free to wander from hotel to hotel, from country to country. He explained in an interview with Hubert Fichte that his errant, rootless existence afforded him great freedom and the possibility for immediate, spontaneous political engagement.

Genet suggests that for the fedayeen, the young male fighters at the forefront of the struggle, landlessness may have a positive effect for it allowed them an availability not unlike his own. The image he suggests is of nomadic warriors who travel from base to base, disappear here and reappear there according to the needs of the moment, and lend themselves to one particular aspect of the struggle or another with ease and grace. Their itinerant existence seems finer still than any of the best *vagabondages* Genet had encountered in Europe: "Strangely enough, Italy which before had seemed so airy, struck me as ponderous compared with the vagabond life of the fedayeen" (*PL*, 314). When two Tunisian friends drive Genet to the desert forty kilometers from Sfax, he is elated by the revelation that tracks in the desert not only linked the network of camps but in fact converged from all of Arabia:

> Then, more seriously, they showed me a place where two tracks met in the sand. One went south with the caravans of female camels, the other went north through Tunisia. Both came from Mauritania, Morocco and Algeria and led to Tripoli, Cairo and the Palestinian camps . . . that was how I learned of the appeal the Palestinian resistance exercised on the Arab nation as a whole, and of the reverberations and almost immediate response it awakened. (*PL*, 15)

Echoing throughout and drawing on different sites and facets of the Arab world, the Palestinian resistance was indeed anything but monolithic. It was in fact highly diverse and fragmented, composed of various subgroups, and, in *Prisoner of Love*, Genet points out with some insistence how it included members of different social classes and even notes the presence of a Black fedayee, Moubarak, originally from the Sudan and educated in English military schools. There were also some Europeans in the midst of Palestinian fighters: French students, German doctors. Furthermore, contributing to a destabilization and multiplication of identity is what Genet calls the flourishing of *noms de guerre* which, similar to the drag queens of *Our Lady of the Flowers* who re-designate their feminine persona, the fedayeen chose for themselves. These names, whose initial function was to conceal the identity of the warriors, now adorn them, Genet notes, and the specific selection of each (such as Castro, Lumumba, Chevara—a contraction of Che Guevara) indicates the fantasies and aspirations of its bearer. Genet compares each pseudonym to a fluid fabric under which one might perceive the reflections of another, and then another: "Khaled just concealed a Maloudi, itself imperfectly covering an Abu Bakr, which again was superimposed on a Kader" (*PL*, 30). The suggestion here is not simply of one identity opaquely concealing an authentic one but of various layers of personality worn almost for pleasure's sake.

Another specific characteristic of the Palestinian struggle derives from the techniques by which it was carried out: with the tactics of guerilla warfare rather than with conventional military strategies. Rather than displaying the upright mechanical allure of a professional army, Genet represents the Palestinians as close to the ground, sinuous in their movements, almost reptilian; and, rather than automatically obeying a chain of command, they are intensely alert to the world around them. To these various manifestations of dynamism, be they traces in the sand or palimpsestic *noms de guerre*, Genet adds another of a religious order. He contrasts to the fixity of Catholicism the mobility and decentralization of Islam, which he represents as multifaceted, open to geographical and historical variation, with a fluctuating religious calendar which designates holidays at different dates on different years: "Instead of the rigidity of Catholicism, Islam offers patterns that are always changing, on earth as in heaven" (*PL*, 156). The highly poetic motif of heavenly patterns is echoed in a very different context in the following passage with the reference to cemeteries in the sky: "Our Palestinian graves have fallen from planes all over the world, with no cemeteries to mark them. Our dead have fallen from one point in the Arab nation to form an imaginary continent" (*PL*, 95). While there might be a material basis to the notion of cemeteries in the sky (where does a landless people bury its dead?), the image is intensely lyrical and connotes lightness, an escape from the fixity, immobility and depth of entombment.

At the same time, the above reference to the tombs fallen from the sky is quite possibly a literal reference to those Palestinians killed during highjackings or suicide bombings. This points to another form of dispersion: the fact that the Palestinians' terrorist actions were not restricted to the actual site of the struggle but often occurred worldwide, since their goal, as in the case of all terrorism, was to shatter complacency, to draw international attention to their cause, and to put the world on alert: "Terrorizing the whole world, making airports put up triumphal arches for us, tinkling like shop doorbells" (*PL*, 95), as a fedayee described it in an improvised chant. An old woman whom Genet visits recites proudly a litany of places where the Palestinians have made themselves known, presumably both through terrorism or by establishing more or less official representation abroad: "We've been in Spain, Holland, France, London (Leila Khaled), Sweden, Norway, Thailand, Germany, Austria. . . . We've been in Italy, Morocco and Portugal" (*PL*, 359). As she speaks she gestures towards an unusual item in a refugee camp, a television set which has brought to her the amazing spectacle of fedayeen in foreign lands. Another Palestinian similarly boasts of the faraway places he has known and the status to which he and his comrades have risen. They have become stars, he brags, and all over the world, in places whose names they hadn't even heard of before, they are the center of the media's attention as journalists swarmed around them in search of photographs and interviews.

As Genet had already observed in the case of the Black Panthers, the media is clearly implicated in this process of glamorization and propagation. Indeed, during the 1970s especially, fedayeen were commonly seen in magazines and on television, and this exposure was responsible for a widespread awareness of the Palestinians' struggle in general and of their actions and threats outside the Middle East in particular. Though the European and American press tended to unanimously decry the acts of violence, it was not without simultaneously glorifying the terrorists, an effect that the fedayeen used to their own advantage, Genet suggests. He quotes one of them: "We automatically adopted a heroic and therefore attractive pose. Legs, thighs, chest, neck—everything helped to work the charm" (*PL*, 10). Very much implicated in the public's fascination for these images was the perceived exoticism of the fedayee's origins: the Arab world has long held captive the European imagination. Furthermore, the guerrilla warfare tactics of this particular struggle were much more easily romanticized than conventional military operations; and the most widely publicized of the Palestinians' actions often involved suicide missions and the kind of dramatic excess that strongly engages the public's emotions. The fedayee quoted above goes on to say that any journalist would have paid dearly to sit at a table with the legendary Carlos (a master terrorist, famous at the time for evading authorities) and have a few drinks with him. Not only would his interview have drawn outstanding magazine sales, but basking in the presence of such a dangerous outlaw would have been very exciting indeed.

The eroticization of criminality and its photographic mediation is something that Genet wrote about much earlier. In the first pages of *Our Lady of the Flowers* the narrator expresses his fascination for the photographs of criminals, which he has cut out of old newspapers and posted on the walls of his prison cell: "These murderers, now dead, have nevertheless reached me, and whenever one of these luminaries of affliction falls into my cell, my heart beats fast" (*OLF*, 52). Known to him only through photographs, these criminals inhabit his imagination, animate his fantasies, and it is in honor of their crimes that he now writes. *The Balcony* also offers an implicit commentary on photography. In this play, the characters' attire does not point to a specific period and its location in time remains purposefully vague. There is one exception: the three young photographers whose jeans and leather jackets are resolutely modern. When these photographers are called upon to fix for eternity the image of the Judge, the Bishop and the General, the play points to the manipulation and artifice involved. The Bishop, for example, is very precisely instructed by the photographer on how to adopt a contemplative air best suited to his functions and given a monocle to hold in place of the holy wafer—on paper their images are indistinguishable, he is told. What Genet is playfully drawing attention to here is the fact that the photographers ultimately control the image they produce—contrary to what the subject might think.

Derived from this is the concern that Genet raised in the case of the Panthers and that he also very much stressed in his writing on the Palestinians: that their struggle might be reduced to a media phenomenon, a spectacle that could be switched on and off in a complete manipulation of the public's interest. Nonetheless, the media's dissemination of images of the Palestinians' struggle was overall enormously helpful to their cause. It is certainly an element that Genet repeatedly draws attention to in a manner that echoes moments in his earlier work and that belongs to the large motif of dispersal under which falls much of his representation of the Palestinians in *Prisoner of Love*. Other facets of this motif are the fedayeen as nomadic warriors, the network of tracks in the desert that indicate the reverberation of the struggle throughout the Arab world, the decentralized tactics of guerrilla warfare and terrorist actions perpetuated on a worldwide scale, all suggesting a revolutionary mode that enchants Genet.

CELEBRATION

On many occasions Genet describes how in the Palestinian military bases there is an atmosphere of lightness, breeziness and ease; its inhabitants interact with a graciousness far beyond mere etiquette and in a manner more conducive to a festive atmosphere than the kind of rigidity that characterizes conventional military hierarchy. The *joie de vivre* that pervades the bases conjures for Genet not-so-distant memories of May '68 in Paris. Indeed, the springtime revolt has been called a *fête* by its supporters and detractors alike and it is true that the students on the street were far from grim. Work was suspended, daily routine (*métro, boulot, dodo*) was replaced by euphoric turmoil. In the passage from *Zoom Magazine* quoted earlier, Genet notes that, similar to the streets of the capital during the student revolt, the Palestinian bases were infused with a joyfulness close to effusion. The crucial difference is that the Palestinians were armed. In the following passage, one of several that draws the analogy, Genet returns to that crucial notion:

> For it was a party, the Palestinian revolt on the banks of the Jordan. A party that lasted nine months. To get an idea of what it was like, anyone who tasted the freedom that reigned in Paris in May 1968 has only to add physical elegance and universal courtesy. But the fedayeen were armed. (*PL*, 247)

This festive, light, breezy atmosphere is quite different from that of the urban enclaves of the Panthers, which Genet depicted in an almost opposite manner: subterraneous, cavernous. He also described the Panthers as implacably serious, whereas on many occasions he writes about the joy and gaiety of the Palestinians. In fact, when he seeks an emblem of unity to hold together the various fragments of the Palestinian revolution, this is what he chooses:

> If I had to use one image for it I'd suggest this . . . .A great yet almost silent roar of laughter from a whole nation holding its sides, yet full of reverence, when Leila Khaled, grenade at the ready, ordered the Jewish crew of the El Al plane to land in Damascus. (*PL*, 162)

Youth and laughter, then, are the common threads of the Palestinian revolution, and this laughter accompanies otherwise deadly serious acts—in this case the famous highjacking of an Israeli plane. The Palestinians' laughter, in this instance, may mark the rejoicing at a moment of triumph and the incongruity of the highjacker (her youth, her gender). On another occasion Genet describes a scene where young girls approach the tanks that enter Amman to besiege the Palestinian population. Among these there is one (a Palestinian) whose gesture of welcome is fake and under whose bouquet a grenade is concealed. Laughing she drops it with the flowers into the tank where it explodes. Here, similarly, the laughter is at the deceit involved, the simplicity of the trick, the contiguity of the gift and the explosive.

Also told to him with laughter was the tale of masquerade of another Palestinian woman, an old woman of eighty this time. Around her fleshless body she had wrapped a string of grenades and, cautiously, amidst conspirational murmurs, with the help of other women accomplices, in what Genet calls funereal and joyous preparations, dressed herself in the most innocuous-seeming clothes. Then, in tears, evoking pity, she crouched in view of enemy soldiers; when her inconsolable laments drew them to gather around, she detonated the explosives. Genet suggests that this action, too, might lead to celebration, for there is no difference between a *fête* and a funeral wake, he notes. All celebrations are steeped in both jubilation and despair, he adds, and, drawing a connection between his current concerns and his earlier works, claims that the words he would use to describe this Palestinian *fête*—nights, forest, septet, jubilation, despair—are "the same words that I would have to use to describe the goings-on at dawn in the Bois de Boulogne in Paris when the drag queens depart after celebrating their mystery doing their accounts and smoothing banknotes out in the dew" (*PL*, 367).

Echoing many suggestions in his earlier work that there exists a correlation between femininity and performance and drawing on these recent instances, Genet claims that women have a particular taste and aptitude for theater, masquerade, impersonation. Throughout *Prisoner of Love* he writes about Palestinian women with warmth and approval. Already, in his writings about the Black Panthers, he had begun to express unprecedented admiration for the women in their midst and in particular bestowed much praise on Angela Davis. He notes that Palestinian women have all the qualities of the men, that they share their wisdom and courage, and that underlying all they do is a great roar of laughter ready to break through and destabilize the surface at any time. Also powerful is the bond between them: in the camps, women take such delight in each other's company that Genet wonders whether the gyneceum was not invented by women rather than men.

To the joyful atmosphere of a *fête*, to the suspension of daily constraints and routines, to playfulness and lightness, Genet adds another element: song, which appears, for example, in a particularly striking episode that occurs four months after Black September, a little before dawn. Echoing through the hills are the improvised chants, responding to one another in turn, of three distinct groups of fedayeen. Genet describes in detail the musicality of the voices—the polyphonic effects, the manner in which, for example, the young ones interact with the mature ones—and ponders their impact on him as they traverse the desert landscape in the darkness. Soon his imagination takes flight: he urbanizes and sexualizes the fedayeen whose camouflage outfits become leopard-print gowns, and with this metamorphosis the possibility of death intrudes:

> It was as if three scattered Queens of the Night, wearing faint mustaches and leopard-print, came together in the morning to carol with the confidence, recklessness and detachment of prima donnas, oblivious of their weapons and their clothes. Oblivious too of the fact that they were really soldiers, who at any moment might be silenced forever by a hail of bullets from Jordan as accurate and melodious as their own singing. (*PL*, 38, *mod*)

Transcending the material signs of their Palestinian fighters' identity (the military dress, the weapons), it is the fedayeen's style and attitude, their proud composure, their careless defiance and haughty indifference that propels them into a metamorphosis, transforms them into worshipped figures of Western high culture: divas of the opera.

Reciprocally, just as the Middle Eastern night allows the metamorphosis of the fedayeen into singing divas, a Parisian night witnesses the transformation of its opera house into a site of Palestinian struggle. This occurred during King Hussein's visit to the French capital; Genet tells of the scene as the motorcade of foreign dignitaries drove up the Avenue de L'Opéra:

> I've been told the gray-green dome [of the Opéra] was the first and perhaps only thing he saw. It had "PALESTINE WILL OVERCOME" painted on it in huge letters. Male dancers, ballerinas and stagehands from the Opéra had gone up on the roof and written the message the night before the procession, and the king saw it. Nowhere in the world seemed safe from the terrorists. (*PL*, 90, *mod*)

The dancers, on this occasion, put their strength and agility to a use other than artistic and, defacing a most venerable building, struck a blow at the predictable pomposity of international diplomacy. One remembers how Genet lamented the fact that the students of May '68 chose to occupy a theater, the one site, he claims, of political inefficacy. Yet, in this instance, the Opéra's imposing monumentality (and ugliness, as Genet does not fail to notice) seems to lend itself quite nicely to the inscription of a political slogan.

PERFORMANCE

Insistently present in Genet's account of the Palestinian struggle and very much linked to several aspects discussed earlier is the element of performance. The performative is clearly at play, for example, when a fedayee photographed by the Western press recounts how he automatically struck a seductive pose for the camera. The slogan "PALESTINE WILL OVERCOME" on the Palais Garnier is inscribed upon a place that symbolizes performance *par excellence*. It is also very much present in the nocturnal chants of the fedayeen echoing through the hills and even more so, of course, in Genet's transformation of the fighters into opera singers. This swift, poetic movement from a Palestinian reality to Western high culture is also central to the following strikingly lyrical passages, taken from the beginning of the book. Shortly after his arrival on the Palestinian bases of northwestern Jordan, not far from the river of the same name, Genet sleeps outdoors and contemplates the night sky:

> The Milky Way rose out of the lights of Galilee and arched over me and the Jordan Valley before breaking up over the desert of Saudi Arabia. Lying there in my blanket I may have entered into the sight more than the Palestinians themselves for whom the sky was a commonplace. Imagining their dreams, for they had dreams, as best I could, I realized I was separated from them by the life I'd lived, a life that was blasé compared with theirs. Cradle and innocence were words so chastely linked, for them, that to avoid corrupting either they avoided looking up. They mustn't see that the beauty of the sky was born and had its cradle in the moving lights of Israel. (*PL*, 7)

There is much at work in this particularly resonant passage. In the opening image, Genet displaces onto stars an illusion commonplace to the folklore surrounding rainbows: the illusion that the arch rises from a particular place on earth—here, a place northwest of the

Palestinian base that Genet chooses to call by its biblical name, Galilee. He then suggests that the Milky Way not only originates there but also draws from the brightness of the land ("out of the lights of Galilee") and that it would be unbearable for the Palestinians to recognize Israel as a source of brightness and light, as the arching configuration of the Milky Way seemingly suggests. The passage contains several possible biblical references (such as the term "cradle" which might connote the birth of Christ) or the idea that stars indicate location (as with Bethlehem to the magi). In the last sentence, as he formulates a fantastical reason for the Palestinian conflict, Genet paradoxically moves away from the biblical term Galilee and designates the land across the Jordan as Israel. He continues:

> In one of Shakespeare's tragedies, the archers lose their arrows against the sky, and I wouldn't be surprised if some of the fedayeen, feet firmly on the ground but angered at so much beauty arching out of the land of Israel, had taken aim and fired their bullets at the Milky Way—China and the socialist countries supplied them with enough ammunition to bring down half the firmament. (*PL*, 7)

Now inspired by a Western literary reference, Genet escalates the idea put forth previously: he imagines the fedayeen expressing anger at the stars—shooting at them. Abruptly interrupting the increasingly poetic and fantastical slant, however, is the reference to a material and political reality: the socialist bloc's support of Palestine. Interestingly, the passage also deploys a strategy often found in Genet's text (and discussed in some detail in the section on camp in the first chapter of this book): the transformation of the serious into the frivolous. One remembers, as an example, a drag queen's claim that the anger expressed the night of the Stonewall riots was due to the recent death of Judy Garland rather than to raging police brutality. Such a transformation is exemplified here when the fedayeen appear angered not by a political reality but by the fact that Israel appears as a source of beauty and innocence. Genet uses this strategy, this transformation of the serious into the frivolous, on many occasions: for example, when he deflates the horror of high-profile terrorist acts such as hijacking, bombing and derailing, reduces them to child's play, to a game of enactment, and suggests that the thrill is because of a spectacular violence done to high-tech objects rather than to human life.

In Genet's subjective and highly poetic recollections of his experiences alongside the Palestinians, recollections more often than not traversed by flights of the imagination, the emphasis on performance is pronounced. But it is not only his literary accounts that allow for this emphasis. Genet suggests that it can sometimes be at the heart of the Palestinians' understanding (or misunderstanding) of their struggle:

> They were committed fighters, inspired by hatred of the enemy and the infamous characteristics attributed to him, the manly pleasure of combat male against male; the satisfaction of bearing aloft the banner of your group. . . . And yet, when the fight was over how was it that none of the dead, whether friend or foe, got up and went and washed the blood off? (*PL*, 339)

It was not, then, that the intensity of the hostility was fake or the very tangible corporeal perception of the fight imagined; on the contrary. Yet the actual deaths ought only to have been enacted; the fedayeen expected a return to neutrality and disengagement after the fighting. Genet goes on to note that he had seen Palestinians capable of anger at Israelis for failing to resurrect, for not adhering to the principle that death should last one night at the very most.

Though the Israelis fail to produce the desired *coup de théatre* and resuscitate once the combat is over, they do not necessarily shy away from theatrics. It appears, in fact, that they, too, rely on performance. One story Genet tells is of a madman who suddenly appeared in West Beirut, living on the streets and sleeping in doorways. The local (Arab) inhabitants soon became used to his crazed antics, to his insane declarations in Arabic with a Palestinian accent, to his vociferous cursing of Israel. He disappears as unexpectedly as he had arrived. Soon after, Israeli tanks entered West Beirut; residents were shocked to recognize the madman in the very first one. He was wearing an Israeli colonel's uniform. Genet's telling of this episode is not without a definite note of approbation for the masquerade and deception involved, even though it was carried out by the opponent.

There is also much admiration expressed for the following event; it was recounted to Genet by a Palestinian friend who himself expressed great awe at the enemy's feat. The story again is of metamorphosis, this time of a group of Israeli soldiers into dizzy drag queens. Genet imagines them: militaristic carriage shaped into a sinuous comportment, blond hair cut in bangs and curls, black eyeliner, scarlet lips. Arms around each other they giddily saunter up towards the highly secured barracks of top-ranking PLO officials. Their loose manner and long kisses soon distract and scandalize but do not threaten the watchful bodyguards who hurl insults. In a split-second about-face, the queens revert back to highly trained marksmen and shoot the guards as well as the key fedayeen. It is with obvious relish that Genet describes this scenario and dwells and embroiders upon the feminization of these very virile soldiers; it is a long and arduous process, he surmises, this transformation not only of the obvious external appearance but of the carriage, the voice—and the kisses, too, had to be practiced. Particularly pleasing to him is the contrast between these long-drawn-out preparations and the instantaneous reversal to military efficacy. He wonders, though, whether once their mission was accomplished, the soldiers had not felt slight regret for the feminine persona they had left behind.

Even though they were carried out by the side with which his sympathies did not lie, these two latter episodes, involving skillful impersonation of madness or the feminine, elicited Genet's admiration. Also very pleasing to him, as mentioned earlier, was the cunning and deceit involved when a young Palestinian woman proffered a fake gesture of welcome and threw into an Israeli tank a bouquet of flowers concealing a grenade; or when the feigned laments of an old woman on a suicide mission drew to her side enemy soldiers among whom she soon detonated the explosives. In all of these cases, performance did not act alone. Rather, it was backed up by and served to enable a more traditional gesture of war, one that involved an intransigent violence and that was as swift as the masquerade was sometimes protracted. Certainly, the Israeli soldiers relied on style to appear as convincing drag queens but also on the very material reality of the guns they concealed. While performance undid rigid boundaries (gender boundaries in the latter case, between friend and foe when the old woman is consoled by enemy soldiers), these were instantaneously reestablished when the illusion disappeared and warfare returned.

There is, however, another far less successful side to performance when it does not belong to a precise strategy and is not followed by military action. Unlike the preceding examples, rather than contribute to the Palestinians' struggle, it can have a detrimental effect and deflate it. Genet points out that on the bases and in the camps, performance was not reserved for spectacular strategic occasions but pervades daily life. Genet shows the epitome of this in a card game that two young fedayeen played in front of a rapt audience, describing how one reached into his pocket for the deck of cards, handed it to his partner to cut, then fanned the cards and shuffled them again before dealing. An intense and concentrated game followed, closely observed by the spectators who sided with one player or another. The cards, however, were nonexistent (considered a product of bourgeois decadence, they were forbidden on the bases). Later, Genet returns to this episode and cautions that this repeated ritual of pretense for its own sake, evening after evening, was not without consequences. It might have encouraged the acceptance of derealization, one that extended to the lost territories. They too became illusory, remaining only as the vaguest and most distant of memories: "As far as I could see, their land—Palestine—was not merely out of reach. Although they sought it as gamblers do cards and atheists God, it had never existed. Vestiges of it remained, very distorted, in people's memories" (*PL*, 107). Perhaps it is for this reason that Genet often says that the Palestinians were not interested in the recovery of territories: these had become unimaginable for them. In any case, he does recognize that the privileging of the performative, however much it might aesthetically please him, can ultimately be detrimental to revolutionary goals. He adds that the players, "fingers full of ghosts, knew that however handsome and sure of themselves they were, their actions perpetuated a card game with neither beginning nor end" (*PL*, 107). However pronounced their apparent competence ("sure of themselves") and aesthetic ("handsome"), what the fedayeens' gestures were lacking was efficiency. Rather than reach a tangible goal that transcended the process, they produced nothing but a repetition itself. While on many occasions he applauded the Palestinians' unconcern for material gains, Genet was also able to regret that in some instances the end became lost.

Genet returns to the notion that the lost territories existed only in vague memories by describing the symbolic reclamation of a Palestinian village near Nazareth. The village had been destroyed by the Israelis and its site reforested. Similar to their disbelief that the Israeli soldiers were really dead, the Palestinians did not accept the fact of their village's destruction and orchestrated its resurrection. Once a year, with their descendants, they gathered at the site to re-create a stylized village very much as one would on a stage. They have brought with them cans of paint, and, on the ground, on tree trunks, on large cloth canvasses stretched between branches, they traced the outline of buildings that once stood. Interestingly, Genet notes that the remnants of that reality, though concealed, were not far beneath the surface: the foundations of the old houses lay beneath a slight layer of dirt. Yet it is the makeshift village that the Palestinians for one day inhabited; it is there that they ate, drank, and told stories of their past home. The elders recounted to the younger ones how things once were, in minute detail at first, then with increasing embellishment and regrets, but ultimately joyfulness and celebration surfaced: "But, gradually, as the imaginary village comes to life, the sadness disappears, and young and old make awkward attempts to dance their ancient dances" (*PL*, 304; *CA*, 408). Though there was celebration, performance and a simulacrum of the lost village, this ritual was void of political efficacy: "For a day, the word resurrection really meant something, and so did nostalgia. This wasn't the sort of longing that precedes the struggle for a real return" (*PL*, 304). At that moment there existed two versions of the mined village. One offered very material traces beneath the surface, invisible but quite possibly perceptible—a fingernail, Genet points out, could have scraped away the soil and revealed the old foundations and cellars. But it was not to these vestiges that the Palestinians paid attention. Rather, they were drawn to what they have represented above ground, the illusory replica, and to its emotive rather than material forms, Genet notes. This version of the village owed its existence to feelings of nostalgia, and its presence is fleeting—it disappeared within a day.

In a rare somber moment of *Prisoner of Love*, Genet laments the predominance of the performative in his own life which he compares to a sheet of paper that can be folded into the myriad shapes—an airplane, a crane—that occupy schoolchildren behind their desk. The sheet of paper, however, holds no shape of its own and, when flat, all that is apparent are the lines where the folds used to be. He remarks that his visible life was "nothing more than well-masked feints," that it was full of gestures that were inflated but of no consequence; it was nothing but a series of imitations of actions, heroic or criminal. He calls himself a "*spontané simulateur*" [spontaneous simulator] and suggests that it is because of this that he was so readily accepted by the Panthers and Palestinians who themselves so much relied on performance:

By agreeing to go first with the Panthers and then with the Palestinians, wasn't I just one more factor of unreality inside both movements? Wasn't I a European saying to a dream: "You are a dream, don't wake the sleeper." (*PL*, 148)

Genet, however, oscillates in typical fashion for elsewhere he emphasizes the importance of his role as witness to the Palestinians, pointing out that his representation of their struggle will far outlive its historical reality. He explains that the fame of heroes has little to do with the extent of their conquests, but, rather, depends on the quality of the tributes paid to them. The Iliad, the Song of Roland, the Colonne Vendôme—it is these images of war that remain for centuries after the actual battles have been forgotten, as will—Genet implies—*Prisoner of Love* long after the Palestinian struggle has subsided.

Conclusion:
1945/1968

IN AN INTERVIEW PUBLISHED IN THE *Revue d'Etudes Palestiniennes* THE
same year as *Prisoner of Love*, Genet has more to say on the status and
significance of his writing. The actual exchange took place in 1984,
in Vienna, where Genet had gone to participate in demonstrations
against the massacres of Sabra and Chatila. He agreed to speak with
a young journalist, Rüdiger Wishenbart, and the conversation
evolved into a long, thorough and illuminating exchange, branching
out in several directions, one of which concerned developments in
Genet's literary and political trajectory. Contrary to what was usually
the case, on this occasion Genet was quite happy to openly and seriously offer his insights on the question. He describes his early literary
production as resulting from a *rêverie* in which, he admits, he had lost
himself to a certain degree. It was only much later, through his involvement with two revolutionary movements, the Panthers and the
Palestinians (in which he intervened, he stresses, only because he was
asked to do so by members of the groups themselves), that he was
able to find himself again: "*Je me suis retrouvé*," he says (*ED*, 277). It was
then that he was able to enter into the realm of action, that he was
able to operate in relation to the real world rather than in relation to
what he calls "the grammatical world." He ponders the difference between the two and points out that while he was writing his books
from prison he was master of his imagination, master of the element
on which he worked. One can act upon *rêverie* in an unlimited manner, he says, but one cannot do the same upon the real; the discipline
required there is entirely different from the grammatical one he had
worked with earlier. There were elements of the real to which he sim-

131

ply had to submit, and, in his new literary production, he had to construct a narrative with ideas that did not necessarily originate with him. But this he did, nonetheless, with his own words, words from the past that remained his. He ends his remarks with the comment: "In my books from thirty years ago, it is not the same writing; but it is the same man talking" (*ED*, 278).

My hope is that the preceding chapters have uncovered, among other things, the ways in which, from Genet's earliest work to his latest, there are consistent and recognizable intonations: the same man talking. One consistency, of course, as I mentioned in the introduction and have referred to throughout my reading, is the oscillation, noted by Sartre, between existentialism and essentialism. There are, too, other suggestive resonances and echoes worth tracing in this concluding section. Take, for example, that quite inescapable component of Genet's early fiction: the dismantling of dichotomies. It is around this particular feature of his aesthetics that Catherine Millot, a French writer and psychoanalytical theorist, in a recent study entitled *Gide, Genet, Mishima: l'intelligence de la perversion*, constructs one of the more interesting analyses of Genet to have appeared in recent decades.[1] She traces the various paradigms through which binary oppositions are undone, such as, for example, the metamorphosis of one extreme into another—metamorphoses, like that of pathos into triumph, in this study's chapter on drag. Another model appears less as a sweeping metamorphosis than as a bringing together and/or movement between two poles: for example, between the sacred and the profane (such as in the description of the priest who makes the sign of the cross with four little shocks of his sprinkler, a sprinkler that "is always moist with a tiny droplet, like Alberto's prick which is stiff in the morning and which has just pissed" [*OLF*, 170]), or between flowers and convicts. For as Genet points out in the opening pages of *The Thief's Journal*, there is a close relationship between the two, and his delight is the oscillation between one and the other. In her examination of Genet's poetic demonstration of the identity of opposites at a point where outside and inside are equivalent, and his remarkable paradoxes of logic that force one to admit that a proposition is both true and false, Millot traces another process which does not simply bring together opposites but sends them into a spiraling circulation where identity and opposites no longer exist. Suggestive of this process is the dizzying sentence describing Divine's death: "in a pool of her vomited blood which was so red that, as she expired,

she had the supreme illusion that this blood was the visible equivalent of the black hole which a gutted violin, seen in a judge's office in
the midst of a hodge-podge of pieces of evidence, revealed with dramatic insistence, as does a Jesus the gilded chancre where gleams His
flaming Sacred Heart" (*OLF*, 57).

While it is true that in Genet's later texts there are fewer moments
of such lyrical intensity, the following sentences from an essay of the
1970s leaves little doubt about certain continuities of style, image
and imagination. Also having to do with death, it was written immediately after George Jackson's assassination. Stylistically and in terms
of imagery, it echoes the preceding passage:

> A few hours after Jackson's death, I had this dream half awake: nine
> months, or a little more, apart, Jonathan and George violently exited
> the prison, womb of stone, amidst streams of blood. This expulsion
> resembled the birth of twins of the same age. . . . George Jackson
> rises again, brushed himself off, now illustrious, that is to say lumi-
> nous, and bearing a light so bright that it designates him and all
> Black Americans.* (*ED*, 111)

Conjunctions of opposites, though perhaps less glaring than in
the early works, inhabit many a page of *Prisoner of Love*. One of the
most obvious, I would suggest, is Genet's insistence that what sets the
Panthers and Palestinians apart from other revolutionaries or rebels
is that they rely both on style (light, breezy and joyful in the Middle
East; darker, subterranean, trenchant in the United States) and on
substance (an armed struggle). One remembers how he applauds
the manner in which the Panthers' project combines seemingly opposed priorities: grassroots practicality on the one hand, far-reaching
revolutionary vision on the other. In his representations of the Palestinians, he shows their landlessness to be both a strength (poetic)
and a weakness (political). His descriptions of the Panthers refer to
the contradictory forces of retinue and attraction that seem to characterize their interactions and note the double edge of tenderness
and violence to their voices; and he does not hesitate to see in David
Hilliard, a Black man much younger than himself, a father. One of
the many things that caused Genet's fascination for George Jackson
was the hybrid nature of *Soledad Brother*, a text whose introduction he
describes as both personal testimony and social commentary, both
manifesto and love poem. Genet also spends much time depicting
how the Palestinian resistance brought together vastly diverse peo-

ple, drawn from social classes high and low and from diverse cultural and even national backgrounds; emblematic of this diversity is the much-loved figure of Mubarak, a Black fedayee from the Sudan who had been educated in British military schools. On many occasions Genet delights in the fact that accompanying the Palestinians' most deadly serious acts were cascades of laughter. He remarks, in *Prisoner of Love*, that "a wake is a kind of a fête. In fact, every fête is at once jubilation and despair" (*PL*, 367). This is yet another moment in his final work that brings us back to the first, to the opening pages of *Our Lady of the Flowers*, to Divine's funeral procession where "the girl queens are huddled together, chattering and chirping around the boy queens" (*OLF*, 59), then to her grave site where they "turned the whole area into a squealing of pretty cries and high giggles" (*OLF*, 70). Setting the tone in an unforgettable manner for the rest of the novel, this episode is far from somber, yet pervaded by a profound and inescapable melancholy.

Among all the different types of undoing of binary oppositions, one stands out as the most powerful and, according to Millot, typical of Gide and Mishima as well as Genet. In fact, in the introduction to her study, she explains that she brings these three authors together not because of their common homosexuality but because of what she calls their shared perversity, a term that refers to their ability to accomplish the greatest miracle of all: to transform suffering into *jouissance* and lack into plenitude. They know the art, she says, "of making virtue out of necessity, and of triumphing over misfortune, which is a matter of style."[2] In her chapter on Genet she considers from a psychoanalytical point of view the mystical and religious aspects of this transformation; her concerns and frame of reference are therefore quite different from mine, yet the process of transformation she refers to is, in and of itself, central to my readings. Indeed, in the chapter on drag I discussed in some detail the metamorphosis whereby passive recipients of external negative circumstances transform their status into that of active and often triumphant agents. One of the purest examples of this often complicated process occurs when the young Louis Culafroy, absorbed in priestlike contemplation, strolling down a park alley in a solemn and dignified manner, suddenly trips but transforms the mishap into a graceful pirouette. Often such transformations occur to transcend shame and humiliation through an excessive production of what brought on ridicule in the first place, in an effort, as Genet wrote of the Carolinas, to pierce the shell of the world's contempt.

Remarkably, Genet's later writing suggests that he perceived very similar mechanisms at work in the revolutionary enterprise of the Black Panthers and the Palestinians. One remembers how much he stresses that the Panthers' greatest victory was their metamorphosis from invisible to visible. Yet, in achieving this metamorphosis, the Panthers used what was the most obvious mark of their difference—skin color—to their advantage. Genet enthuses: "Against a black skin, light or dark, matching tones or contrasts of gold and azure, pink and mauve, are all equally striking" (*PL*, 84). Because of their unapologetic self-presentation, he adds, the Panthers not only made themselves visible but, far from being a uniform mass of darkness, made themselves luminous. Furthermore, while in general they did not invest in an African identity, did not surround themselves with the folkloric artifacts of a long lost past, when it came to their hair they strongly rejected attempts to conform to European standards. Neither artificially straightened or plastered down into a subdued shape, its singularity was taken to extremes with wide and tall afros, a style that White Americans reacted to with trepidation. Indeed, because it amplified rather than reduced difference and no doubt because it exceeded the boundaries of the conventional Western body, this halo of hair was perceived as aggressive: "When the Panthers' afro haircut hit the whites in the eye, the ear, the nostril and the neck, . . . they were panic-stricken. How could they defend themselves . . . against all this vegetation, this springing, elastic growth . . . ?" (*PL*, 218).

When dark complexions are no longer simply endured but used in a colorful visual effect that just cannot be ignored, or when an enormous afro is made to provoke unease in fellow subway riders, what is suggested is an excessive production of attributes that were the object of America's scorn in the first place. It coincides perfectly with the Carolinas' rapturous cries and high-pitched giggles aimed at piercing the shell of the world's contempt. One might also wonder whether this mechanism is not reminiscent, in some ways, of other strategies of Black liberation, from negritude to Black Nationalism. The difference, at least in Genet's perception, is that the Panthers' self-presentation did not serve primarily to form bonds and ensure cohesion within the group. Rather than merely a statement of identity it was used as a weapon very much directed at the outside world.

I noted in the chapter on drag that transformations of passive objects of scorn into triumphant subjects could be viewed as revolts against falsely naturalized and impermeable boundaries. In Genet, these are most often corporeal, but can be national as well. Indeed, expulsed from their homeland, scattered among various sites in no country that truly welcomes them, the Palestinians, Genet suggests, are able to transform this lack into an advantage: landlessness is a virtue for it allows them an availability not unlike his own. The fedayeen, transcending a status of passive victims relegated to refugee camps, transformed their forced displacement into a chosen and strategic mobility. Genet notes how they sprung up all over the globe—as official PLO representatives here, as terrorist commandos there, showing up especially in places and circumstances where they would least be expected. Their images were reproduced by the media throughout the world at large. "We've been in Spain, Holland, France, London, Sweden, Norway, Thailand, Germany, Austria. . . . We've been to Italy, Morocco and Portugal" (*PL*, 359), an elderly woman proudly announces, gesturing towards her television screen. This last example of the transformation of homeless refugees into nomadic warriors who, having lost their homeland, are willing to circle the globe and give up their very lives for the struggle is one of many such transformations in Genet's representation of both the Panthers and the Palestinians.

In relation to these instances of metamorphoses of passive victims into active agents, one cannot help but recall again what surely counts as one of the most memorable passages in Genet's political texts. I am referring to the passage in "The Assassination of George Jackson" where Genet describes the life of the revolutionary as a struggle against a false fatalism: "I think that one must not refuse revolutionaries, when it becomes necessary to them, this sort of magnificence of reverie and act, above all when the act must become exemplary, that is, when it serves to show, brilliantly, the meaning and direction of a life that has striven to be a thorough struggle against a false fatalism"* (*ED*, 116).

This struggle, which certainly takes place against falsely naturalized boundaries and subject position, was undertaken with equal flamboyance by his drag queens of the '40s and freedom fighters of the '70s. In passing, though, one might note that no such struggle was undertaken by Genet's maids of the '50s. I am of course referring here to the play, to Leo Bersani's brilliant analysis in *Homos* (a work I refer to in greater detail later), and in particular to his remark that the "Maids' dilemma is that there is nothing they might do to Madame that would not confirm their identity as maids."[3] Indeed, their efforts oscillate between a desire to be Madame and a desire to annihilate her but certainly do not include a desire to exacerbate their own specificity. Fortunately for the reader of Genet's late works, those of the Panthers and Palestinians did.

The disruption of binary oppositions and the transformation of victim into agent are not the only features present in both Genet's early and late works. From the pages of *Our Lady of the Flowers* to those of *Prisoner of Love* surfaces a style known as camp which I discussed earlier in the chapter on drag, noting that its chief characteristics are that it represents life as theater, that it transforms the serious into the frivolous and that it celebrates excess. Strikingly, all three features of this style, which of course is at its most intense in Genet's representation of drag queens, are also present in his depictions of revolutionaries. One remembers that drag involved an excessive display of feminine style, evident, for example, in Divine's gestures (the enormous arc), her language (ripples of flowers escape from her mouth) and adornments, such as the Persian miniature painstakingly painted on her fingernails. My earlier discussion of Genet's representation of the Panthers' hair and dress suggests such excess, which is equally present in other aspects of what he views as their revolutionary style. Indeed, referring not only to their physical appearance but also to their ever-inflated and unavoidably seductive rhetoric and to the startling effects of their public demeanor and comportment, Genet writes: "Excess in display, in words, in attitude, swept the Panthers to ever greater excess" (*PL*, 85). As was the case when Divine was mocked by young boys then reduced them to silence when she displayed her outrageously ornate hands, this excess captivates the gaze of others and commands attention. Indeed, it is because of their embrace of excess that the Panthers, no longer reducible to a silent mass of darkness, made what according to Genet was the greatest transformation of all: from invisible they became visible and invaded White consciousness.

Yet another element of camp, performance, pervades the pages of *Prisoner of Love*. Many examples come to mind—such as his descriptions of the Panthers' life as a performance upon which a curtain never falls, or of the fedayee who, when photographed by the press, immediately strikes a heroic pose. Genet also delights in recounting various ploys that all involve a certain degree of masquerade—such as that of the old woman, who, appearing pitiful and despondent, attracted the sympathy of soldiers, only to detonate a bomb among them as they huddled to comfort her, or of the young girl who in an apparent gesture of welcome threw into an enemy tank a bouquet that concealed a grenade. Also very much related to the idea of performance and also bringing queens and revolutionaries together are the drag names and *noms de guerre*. In both *Our Lady of the Flowers* (where he playfully refers to the queens' convoluted names as *noms de guerre*) and *Prisoner of Love* Genet uses the term "adornment" to describe the function of these names, and, in both cases, reflects on their origin. In the case of drag names he points out that there is "a kinship among them, an odor of incense and melting taper, and I sometimes feel as if I had gathered them among artificial flowers in the Chapel of the Virgin Mary" (*OLF*, 282). Those of the revolutionaries are evocative, too, pointing either to political greatness (Lumumba, Che Guevara) or, on a much more frivolous note, to the unlikely seduction of Hollywood, taken "from garbled memories of American films" (*PL*, 30). A significant difference, though, is that, in *Our Lady of the Flowers*, at Our Lady's trial the intervention of the state is one that succeeds in divesting the queens of their identity and uncovering an "identité civile" [a civilian identity] that remains the official and untouchable record: "Our Lady saw Mimosa II enter. The clerk, however, had called out 'René Hirsch.' When he called 'Antoine Berthollet,' First Communion appeared; at 'Eugène Marceau,' Lady-apple appeared. Thus, in the eyes of Our bewildered Lady, the little faggots from Pigalle to Place Blanche lost their loveliest adornment, their names lost their corolla" (*OLF*, 281). The stateless fedayeen, however, who are submitted to no law, need not fear this uncovering of an irreducible and banal self: "Khaled just concealed a Maloudi, itself imperfectly uncovering an Abu Bakr, which again was superimposed on a Kader" (*PL*, 30). The suggestion here is not of one identity opaquely concealing an authentic one but, even more powerfully, of fluid and coreless layers.

The remark that inspiration for the fedayeen's *noms de guerre* came from world revolutionaries or from Hollywood actors points to another important feature of camp: the co-existence of the serious and the frivolous and, often, the transformation of the one into the other. Such a co-existence occurs in "Quatres heures à Chatila," the text that describes in painful detail the mutilated and decaying corpses of Palestinian refugees murdered by right-wing Christian Lebanese militias. Towards the end, almost flippantly, Genet makes this remark, which appears to minimize the political stakes of the Algerian revolution and in its place emphasizes the aesthetic: "One should accept the evidence: [the Algerians] liberated themselves politically to appear such as one should view them: very beautiful" (*ED*, 261). Much earlier, in *The Thief's Journal*, Genet had described a group of queens making a pilgrimage to the site of a destroyed urinal, in a solemn procession, to lay there a wreath of roses—a dignified treatment of a less than monumental site. Similarly, in *Prisoner of Love*, Genet recounts how a group of displaced Palestinians also make a pilgrimage but in remembrance of a much more tragic loss: that of their village now completely erased. Yet there is something astonishingly playful and lighthearted in the ceremonial: with paint, on tree trunks, on the ground, on canvases hung between branches, they trace the outline of buildings as they once stood, then dance and drink and tell of the past. Elsewhere, Genet tells of the nocturnal, improvised chants of fedayeen who, instead of discreetly holding guard or silently surveying a scene, set aside all military seriousness and could not resist making themselves known through song: "[They] carol with the confidence, recklessness and detachment of prima donnas, oblivious of their weapons and their clothes. Oblivious too of the fact that they were really soldiers who at any moment could be silenced forever by a hail of bullets from Jordan" (*PL*, 38).

Genet suggests a similar sensibility when he imagines a fedayee firing at the stars, angered not by a political reality but by the fact that the milky way appears to have its source in Israel. He repeatedly describes the lighthearted, festive atmosphere of the camps and is quite specific in his analogy between queens and revolutionaries when he notes that the very words he uses to depict the strongholds of the fedayeen are those that would be equally appropriate to describe certain areas of the Bois de Boulogne, a well-known haunt of transvestites: "Of course it's understood that the words night, forest, septet, jubilation, desertion and despair are the same words that I have to use to describe the goings-on at dawn in the Bois de Boulogne in Paris when the drag queens depart after celebrating their mystery, doing their accounts and smoothing their bank notes out in the dew" (*PL*, 367).

One vital difference, though, between Genet's use of camp in his early and late works has been commented upon by Marie Redonnet in *Jean Genet, le poète travesti*.[4] This work, written not by a literary critic but by a fellow novelist and playwright, is designed as a reflection on what the author considers to be one of the greatest questions of our time—the relationship between poetry and revolution. Her analyis, though taking place in a tangential and somewhat convoluted manner, suggests that poetry has the advantage (which some would regard as dubious) of remaining intact even after revolutions fail. Nonetheless, Redonnet's seductive text, often highly poetical itself, does succeed in offering elegant and insightful musings over certain moments of Genet's drama and prose. One such enlightening moment occurs in the following remark: "The magic existed because women also became liberated and incarnated this new beauty. Through revolutionary magic Genet has liberated himself from an exclusively masculine beauty and leaves his homosexual prison."[5]

While Redonnet's term "homosexual prison" is questionable (though used by Genet himself in "Fragments"), her description of the process is accurate and well put. It is indeed the case that camp in the early work functions in the representation of a performative feminine style, while biological women are treated with derision if not disgust. In later works, where camp is at the service of revolution, such derision is no longer to be found. Indeed, starting with his texts on the Panthers, Genet wrote warmly of the women among their midst and in *Prisoner of Love* represents Palestinian women in the most positive of terms: he claims that while sharing the men's wisdom and courage they participate more fully in the festive aspect of the revolution as well as in its theatrics (the old woman with explosives concealed under her dress, the young girls welcoming enemy soldiers with the toss of a grenade).

It appears, then, that in the texts where camp is displaced from queens to revolutionaries, women are shown in a much more generous light than previously. Along with this acceptance there seems to be in the later works a lesser degree of pessimism and despair, a pessimism that emerged quite regularly in the early novels, such as when, in the scene at Our Lady's trial, the queens lose their glorious names and Genet goes on to describe them as "misery in motley" (*OLF*, 281). Marie-Claude Hubert in *L'Esthétique de Jean Genet*, a work that offers subtle and compelling analyses of Genet's imagery, cites a similar moment in *Miracle of the Rose*: the narrator suddenly sees the prison divested of its poetic aura, of its glorious attributes, and is cruelly marked by its unadorned nakedness.[6] She notes that such fleeting moments of the pessimism of the 1940s are premonitory of a trend that became much more explicitly expressed in a short text of 1967.[7] At its core is the expression of a realization profoundly distressing to Genet: that he might be just like any other man. This awareness came to him, he explains, when traveling on a train. He became repulsed by the sight of a particularly unattractive old man, then suddenly was traversed by the unsettling knowledge that he himself, all of his quests for singularity through art notwithstanding, was no different from his unfortunate companion. The effect of this realization was profound: his impression was that everything around him became disenchanted and began to rot. Hubert argues, and quite convincingly, that Genet's turn towards the political was prefigured by this aesthetic disinvestment. A remarkable aspect of Genet's work, I would add, is that neither the Panthers nor the Palestinians undergo this process of disenchantment. The fedayeen's *noms de guerre* does not reveal a bland core of authenticity, and when Genet, in his May Day speech, makes the lucid effort to view Bobby Seale's jail in realist rather than poetic terms, he sees it as stone and steel but never sordid and its inhabitants never anything less than splendid.

While, then, these concluding remarks suggest that between the early and late Genet there are significant differences and many continuities (the undoing of binary oppositions, the passage from passive victim into active agent, the emphasis on performance, the transformation of the serious into the frivolous, the cultivation of excess), the importance of the major shift brought on by the awakening of Genet's political concerns cannot be overly emphasized. This shift, as I mentioned in the opening page of this conclusion, is one that Genet himself described as occurring between a world of *rêverie*, in which his imagination dominated, and one in which he had to submit to elements of the real. In an article written immediately after the publication of *Prisoner of Love* in 1986 and published in a special issue of the *Revue d'etudes Palestiniennes*, Félix Guattari points out that immediately after making that distinction Genet erodes it to some extent (saying that "everyone knows that reverie belongs to the real world, dreams are reality").[8] Yet, I would argue that his initial statement remains in fact quite valid. As I mentioned in the chapter on the Panthers, Genet's first wave of political articles was grounded in the factual. In these, following what he said in his May Day speech, he made conscious choices to ensure that no unreality crept into his statements—suggesting that it required a concerted effort on his part to keep *rêverie* at bay. This may very well be because, as Guattari points out in his psychoanalytically informed article, "Genet never did cross the threshold that allows one to adapt to reality [*n'aura jamais franchi le seuil d'adaptation au réel*]" and hence displays a "subjective disposition able to revive waves of imaginary vehicled by reality." It remains, however, that reality does play a greater role in the focus and organization of his later work, even if in the second set of articles and in *Prisoner of Love* poetic license is alive and well. As Guattari puts it, Genet was remarkably able to remain profoundly attached to his infantile perversions and dreams while at the same time engaging in a most lucid manner with adult and contemporary realities. He goes so far as to suggest that his early works reach beyond the purely literary: "It is true that the creative process, in Genet, has always involved fabulation—masturbatory or not—but its fundamental aim remains a socially relevant poetics. The writing of his early texts is inseparable from the penitentiary condition."[9]

In light of Genet's trajectory towards social engagement and of the resonances that exist between his early and late work, it is legitimate to wonder whether, retrospectively, it might not be possible to give a more political reading to his early texts. I would disagree with Guattari's particular argument, however, that the mere fact that the early novels are written in and to some extent about jail suggests that they are socially relevant. More attractive is the position held by Leo Bersani in *Homos*, a work that stems from its author's reactions, both favorable and unfavorable, to the current discrediting on the part of self-defined homosexual activists and theorists of anything resembling what is often and not without some derision termed "identity politics." *Homos* also appears to stem from Bersani's weariness towards the far too zealous efforts of gays and lesbians to be good citizens, as they strenuously prove that they can be "good parents, good soldiers, good priests." In sharp contrast to what he calls the current rage of respectability are works by the three authors that he examines—Gide, Genet, Proust. From his reading of these works, he suggests that a politically disruptive aspect of homosexuality is "a gay desire to redefine sociality so radical that it may appear to require a provisional withdrawal from relationality itself."[10] It is mainly to Genet's *Funeral Rites* that Bersani turns to make this point, but it seems to me that most of Genet's early works might display such a withdrawal from relationality or, as Bersani calls it elsewhere in the same text, an anticommunitarian impulse. He suggests that Genet's novels (along with works by Gide and Proust) demonstrate how desire for the same can affect a liberation from an oppressive psychology of desire-as-lack and achieve "a salutary devalorizing of difference—or, more exactly, a notion of differences not as trauma to be overcome (a view which, among other things, nourishes antagonism between the sexes) but rather as a non-threatening supplement to sameness."[11] While there is no doubt that Sartre would reject this temporary withdrawal from sociality as an infantile (and bourgeois) pastime, rather than a strategy that might lead to useful political change, I would argue that it is quite possible that Genet's early works, by effecting this "temporary withdrawal" (granted, a rather long temporary withdrawal, but one from which he did finally emerge) from the social, aided in the evacuation of a bourgeois notion of difference as trauma, which surely nourishes antagonism between races as well as between sexes. One might consider that this process indeed facilitated Genet's later relationship with the Palestinians (whose cause Edward Said judges to be the only one not co-opted in the West by liberal or dominant ideology) and the Panthers (whose struggle, Genet noted, no other White intellectual was prepared to join).

While I doubt Guattari's point that Genet's representation of incarceration automatically meant that his texts were socially relevant, I do entirely agree with what in fact is the premise of my own study: that "Sartre's mausoleum reveals itself rather poorly suited to the stature that Genet ultimately revealed" and that he was wrong to have condemned Genet "to remain circled by an imaginary fed by a malignant phantasmagoria."[12] One might, in these final pages, offer a few clues as to why Sartre got it wrong. A first reason, which I briefly alluded to in the introduction, has to do with Sartre's reactions to World War II. Whereas for Genet there was a pre- and post-1968, for Sartre there was a pre- and post-1940. The terms that Denis Hollier in *The Politics of Prose: Essay on Sartre* borrows to describe this shift sound very much like those used by Genet in his Wishenbart interview with *rêverie* and imagination on the one hand and reality on the other:

If we can believe the version that he himself broadcast rather generously, Sartre would have more or less continued to slumber and

dream until 1940. That was the year in which the frontier that his
philosophical works had traced between the real and the imaginary
would finally traverse his life, which it cut in two. Before 1940, he was
living in the unreal; starting in 1940, he began to perceive: "The war
opened my eyes," he says in *On a raison de se révolter.*[13]

Not so for Genet: throughout the war he will remain (in and out
of jail) shrouded in *rêverie,* master of his imagination. Granted, the
occupation, nazism, even Hitler find a place in *Funeral Rites* but
hardly in a way that might have given Sartre much hope. While it is
not entirely true that Genet was oblivious to World War II, he did not
seize this occasion to engage in the social but rather appropriated
the conflict to fuel a text where memory and fantasy distort each
other as the narrator succumbs to an orgiastic proliferation of desires that cross enemy lines to include a German soldier and a member of the French militia. In *Funeral Rites,* the erotic fantasies the
narrator spins around these two figures emerge at a specific moment
in time, the funeral of his young lover ("that twenty-year-old communist who, on August 19, 1944, was picked off the barricades by the
bullet of a charming young collaborator" [*FR,* 17]), and constitute a
reaction to a specific emotion: his revulsion at seeing his own memories of his lover tainted and trivialized by a collective ritual that is
being made to serve a patriotic cause that he despises. One of the
most striking aspects of these erotic fantasies is that they include
what one might term an eroticization of fascism, embodied to a large
extent by the representations of the German soldier. In the numerous representations of this soldier's body, there appear to be two em-
phases: one focusing on its sheer muscularity and power, the other
highlighting its angularity and frozen poses. The attention to the soldier's physical prowess finds its corollary in the nazi cult of strong,
athletic bodies and its adulation of brute, physical force. Yet this aesthetic is not necessarily bound to a fascist context; it appears time
and time again in Genet's other works. Further, as I discussed in the
second chapter of this study, Genet's male bodies are often shown
striking single, motionless poses—in stark contrast to the queens.
When they do move, it is in a controlled, mechanical manner. In
"Fascinating Fascism," Susan Sontag draws attention to fascist archi-
tecture's blunt massing of the material, sharp lines and "petrified
eroticism," terms very similar to those in which Genet describes desired male characteristics. Sontag further remarks that fascist style is

one that privileges a "congealed, static, virile, posing" and "movements are confined, held tight, held in."[14] There exists, then, a correlation between certain aspects of a fascist aesthetic and what Genet represents as desirable male bodies. However, it is important to realize that his attraction to this particular corporeal style predates, by far, his encounter with fascist Germany. It can no doubt be traced to a period he himself views as formative of his sexuality, namely, the time he spent as a youngster in the Mettray reformatory, where boys were clad in austere uniforms and shorn to the skull. Daily life in the institution had a Spartan, paramilitary quality to it and was organized according to a strict hierarchical order with the boys etching tattoos into one another's skin to indicate their status. In "The Criminal Child," a censored radio broadcast, Genet looks back on his days at Mettray, a place "where cruelty and violence are the poetic expressions of the youngsters' affirmation of evil and rebellion," with great nostalgia and explains that he experienced emotions so strong that his life was indelibly marked by them.[15] The militarization of French life during the occupation no doubt brought back to Genet certain aspects of his reformatory experience and this at a time when Germany had roundly defeated the country he loathed. It is then not in the least surprising that he would find in a German soldier an especially alluring object of desire. Most important, though, one must realize that this work cannot be taken to seriously express a political position. Bersani, in *Homos*, makes this clear: "With its casually obscene treatment of Hitler as an old queen, the work could hardly be picked up as an advertisement for nazism. With its frequent shifts of tone and subject position . . . *Funeral Rites* is constantly reminding us that identities and convictions cannot be assigned, in fantasies, to particular persons."[16] In fact, *Funeral Rites* is the very work that Bersani chooses to epitomize what I discussed earlier: Genet's "fundamental project of declining to participate in any sociality at all."[17]

I would argue, then, that it is to a large extent because Genet did not participate in the widespread political awakening brought on by World War II that Sartre judged him irrecuperable. There is another reason for Sartre's misjudgment, a reason that helps further clarify Genet's reactions to the war. One remembers that in *Saint Genet* Sartre isolates one defining moment that, he believes, will shape the rest of Genet's life: the moment when, as a child, he is named a thief and from then on will attempt to actively embody and exacerbate this identity. There is an equally, if not more, defining moment that

Genet himself identifies in his interview with Fichte:

> Let me remind you that I have neither father nor mother, that I was brought up by the welfare system, in foster homes, and that I found out very young that I was not French, that I did not belong to the village . . . I found it out in a dumb way, just like that: the schoolteacher had asked each of us to describe our house, It just so happened that my description was, according to the schoolteacher, the prettiest. He read it out loud and everybody made fun of me, saying "but that's not his house! he's an abandoned child!" and there was such a void, such humiliation. I was immediately made so foreign, oh! the word is not too strong, to hate France, that's nothing, more than vomit France, anyway . . .[18]

This sentiment, which Genet echoes in several other interviews, is particularly significant here—the moment of humiliation is one that accompanies a recognition of the superior quality of his writing. This moment and Genet's distaste for and distrust of French society which follows are equally, if not more, determining than the moment when he was defined as a thief. A similar view is expressed by the French philosopher Hadrien Laroche in *Le Dernier Genet*, a commentary on the last eighteen years of Genet's life.[19] He emphasizes the significance of this moment of rejection in the orphan's childhood and views Genet's *oeuvre* as follows: "His life and work are entirely contained in this conjunction between a childhood with political consequences and then a political engagement that fulfills the void of childhood."[20]

Sartre, I would suggest, did not realize what the consequences of Genet's rejection from property-owning French patriarchy might be: during World War II, when worker and bourgeois united (apparently) against a common enemy, Genet remained an outcast. However, in May '68, when France turned against itself, Genet was delighted: "In May, the France that I hated so much no longer existed" (*ED*, 41), he explains later in an interview. This moment, clearly, opened up a potential in a manner that Sartre did not foresee, and Genet's soon-to-follow connection with the Panthers and Palestinians allowed him to finally participate in a previously impossible sociality (to retain Guattari's term)—or to put it another way—it was the Panthers and Palestinians who allowed the historicization and politicization of Genet's poetics. One remembers how Genet in his very first work, *Our Lady of the Flowers*, comments on the nature of poetry and explains that "[poetry] was born, for example, on Saturdays, when, to clean the rooms, housewives put the red velvet chairs, gilded mirrors, and mahogany tables outside, in the nearby meadows" (*OLF*, 226). In *Prisoner of Love*, one finds a strikingly similar yet significantly different passage just a few pages before the end of the book:

> I was always delighted when furniture symbolizing wealth and comfort was put to derisory uses. One night by the light of the moon, on a dry and stony bit of land between Ajloun and Irbid, I found myself in the middle of a conclave of high-backed Voltaire chairs. It was March 1971, and all the fedayeen on the base were living in the handful of villas the king had built for his ministers. In a few hours the villas were emptied of these thirty-odd velvet armchairs, which now stood in a circle in a ploughed field. (*PL*, 372)

In its second version, replacing the fairy-tale-like vagueness of "housewives" and "a meadow, " the same image is historicized. It occurs six months after Black September during the aftermath of the bloody conflict between Jordanians and Palestinian refugees and emerges at a precise geographical location: among the cluster of bases just south of the Golan. The actual furniture, too, is historicized: in the first, the chairs are simply red velvet; in the second they are more specifically bourgeois: high-backed Voltaire, also velvet (and one does imagine them red). The first are simply displaced from inside to outside. In the second, they are not only twice displaced, each displacement involves an appropriation: first from its French bourgeois origins to the Arabic aristocracy, then from the Arabic aristocracy to the Palestinian fedayeen. The poetic core remains the same: its context and repercussions are widely different. The chairs are no longer standing midday among the lushness of the French countryside but in a ploughed field under the light of a Middle-Eastern moon. The purpose they now serve is revolutionary, and, at the same time, their presence on this "dry and stony bit of land" fulfills the quest outlined in the manuscript note at the top of the final proofs of Genet's final work: "Put all the images of language somewhere safe and make use of them, for they are in the desert, and it's in the desert we must go and look for them" (*PL*, VI, *mod*).

Notes

Notes to Introduction

1. Pascale Gaitet, *Political Stylistics* (New York: Routledge, 1992).

2. Hélène Cixous, "The Laugh of the Medusa," trans. Keith Cohen and Paula Cohen, *Signs* (Summer 1976): 245–66.

3. Jean Genet, *Our Lady of the Flowers*, trans. Bernard Frechtman (New York: Grove, 1987). All further references appear in the text under the abbreviation *OLF. Funeral Rites*, trans. Bernard Frechtman (New York: Grove Press, 1969). All further references appear in the text under the abbreviation *FR*.

4. Jean Genet, *The Thief's Journal*, trans. Bernard Frechtman (New York: Grove, 1973). All further references appear in the text under the abbreviation *TJ*.

5. Julia Kristeva, *Revolution in Poetic Language*, trans. Margaret Waller (New York: Columbia University Press, 1984).

6. Cixous, "The Laugh of the Medusa," 254.

7. Jean Genet, *L'Ennemi déclaré* (Paris: Gallimard, 1991). All further references appear in the text under the abbreviation *ED*.

8. Jean Genet, *Prisoner of Love*, trans. Barbara Bray (Hanover: Wesleyan University Press, 1992). All further references appear in the text under the abbreviation *PL*.

9. Jean-Paul Sartre, *Saint Genet: Actor and Martyr*, trans. Bernard Frechtman (New York: George Braziller, 1963).

10. According to Edmund White in *Jean Genet: A Biography* (New York: Knopf, 1993), Sartre was initially wary of Jean Cocteau's "discovery" in Genet of a great writer, but he was won over by the passages from *Our Lady of the Flowers* that were published in *L'Arbalète* in 1944. The two met soon after and conversed regularly during the following years. In fact, much of Sartre's massive tome on Genet, published in 1952 at the height of Sartre's popularity, was based on these conversations. A closeness developed between the two, so much so that Simone de Beauvoir notes in *La Cérémonie*

des adieux that Genet and Alberto Giacometti were the two most important characters in Sartre's life. In earlier memoirs, she comments on what might have drawn Sartre and Genet together: "The whole basis of Genet's fellowship for Sartre was this whole idea of liberty they shared, which nothing could suppress, and their common adherence of all that stood in its way: nobility of soul, spiritual values, universal justice, and other such lofty words and principles, together with established institutions and ideals" (*La Force de l'âge* [Paris: Gallimard, 1969], 595). As well as from conversations with the author, Sartre drew his material for *Saint Genet* from those works published up to that point: the five prose works, *Our Lady of the Flowers, Miracle of the Rose, Funeral Rites, Querelle* and *The Thief's Journal,* and to a lesser extent the poems, *Chants Secrets,* and the play *The Maids.* Printed secretly by Paul Morihien and Robert Denoel, *Our Lady of the Flowers* began to circulate in 1943 without the mention of a publisher. *Miracle of the Rose* was initially published by L'Arbalète in 1946 and *The Maids* in 1947. That same year, Gallimard issued a clandestine and anonymous publication of *Funeral Rites* and Morihien did the same for *Querelle.* All were later published by Gallimard as *The Complete Works.*

11. Jean-Paul Sartre, *Search for a Method,* trans. Hazel Barnes (New York: Knopf, 1963).

12. Jean Genet, *Miracle of the Rose,* trans. Bernard Frechtman (New York: Grove, 1967). All further references appear in the text under the abbreviation *MR. Querelle,* trans. Anselm Hollo (New York: First Evergreen Edition, 1987). All further references appear in the text under the abbreviation *Q. The Maids,* trans. Bernard Frechtman (New York: Grove, 1954).

13. See White, *Jean Genet,* 335.

14. In what surely must appear as one of the most astonishing aspects of the *Saint Genet* (and of Sartre's Baudelaire as well as his study of Flaubert) is that he does not hesitate in equating Genet with any narrator or character of his texts.

15. See, for example, Jean-Paul Sartre, *The Age of Reason,* trans. Eric Sutton (New York: Knopf, 1966).

16. Simone de Beauvoir, *The Second Sex,* trans. H. M. Parshley (New York: Knopf, 1953).

17. Ibid., 387.

18. In "Is the Rectum a Grave?" (*October* 43 [1987]: 197–216).

Leo Bersani criticizes Altman's assertion that gay baths created a "sort of Whitmanesque democracy, a desire to know and trust other men in a type of brotherhood far removed from the male bondage of rank, hierarchy and competition that characterizes much of the outside world." Dennis Altman, *The Homosexualization of America: The Americanization of the Homosexual* (New York: St. Martin's Press, 1982); see, for example, the baths scene in Robert Gluck, *Jack the Modernist* (New York: Gay Presses of New York, 1995).

19. Jean Genet, Interview by Hubert Fichte (Frankfurt and Paris: Qumran Verlag, 1981), 38.

20. Jean Genet, *The Blacks,* trans. Bernard Frechtman (New York: Grove, 1960); *The Screens,* trans. Bernard Frechtman (New York: Grove, 1963).

21. See White, *Jean Genet,* 481.

22. As Edmund White vividly recounts, many others also viewed it as a play against France, and, when it was first represented, the right wing was irate, particularly because of a hilarious scene where a dead French army officer is saluted by the farts of his men. At several of the first performances, commandos led by—among others—Jean-Marie Le Pen (later to be the leader of the neo-nazi Front National) blocked the entrance to the theater, stormed the stage, ignited smoke bombs and chanted "Down with Genet! Genet the fag!" while leftist students shouted back, "Fascism will not get past us!" Roger Blin, the director, recalls that, in front of such commotion, "Genet died laughing." See White, *Jean Genet,* 492–94.

23. Ibid., 566.

24. Jacques Derrida, *Glas,* trans. John P. Leavy, Jr. and Richard Rand (Lincoln and London: University of Nebraska Press, 1986).

25. In *Dissemination* Derrida refers to this technique as "The Double Session"; there, the texts of Plato and Mallarmé are juxtaposed. Jacques Derrida, *Dissemination,* trans. Barbara Johnson (London: Athlone Press, 1981).

26. As Sartre points out in *Search for a Method,* Marx considered social evolution to be a natural process governed by laws that do not depend upon the will, the conscious intention of men—men who are the passive product of the social conditions under which they live. To this extent, one can consider marxism as a deterministic philosophy. In fact, as Andrew Ross points out in *Universal Abandon* (Minneapolis: University of Minnesota Press, 1988), the marxist notion of a stable class identity is an essentialist one, and, as Sartre points out, it denies the subject its agency in the elaboration of such an identity.

27. George Jackson, *Soledad Brother: The Prison Letters of George Jackson* (New York: Coward-McCann, 1970).

NOTES TO CHAPTER 1

1. There is a certain perversity in such attitudes, of course. In the name of agency, Divine ultimately chooses inactivity and the Carolinas seem to expose themselves to the mocking eye in utmost vulnerability, for the choice involved is invisible to the onlooker who sees Divine as merely weak and the queens as pathetically, hysterically outrageous. Control does not reveal itself as such. I discuss this further in the next section of this chapter.

2. See Sartre's analysis of this "insurmountable contradiction": how can Genet decide to be what he already is? *Saint Genet*, 59.

3. Jean Genet, "Fragments," in *Fragments . . . et autres textes* (Paris: Gallimard, 1990), 77. "Fragments" was first published in 1954 in Sartre's *Les Temps modernes*. Translations of this text are mine.

4. Louis Culafroy is the name of the boy Divine once was.

5. Genet rarely uses the word *travesti* [transvestite] for his drag queens, but calls them *folles* [drag queens] or *tantes* [queens].

6. Part of Our Lady's ambiguity is because he has been given such a name, even though he is not a drag queen.

7. This coolness is phonetically transcribed in the sentence beginning with "In the big café": "*Dans le grand café aux vitres baissées, rideaux tirés sur leurs tringles creuses, surpeuplé, et sombrant dans la fumée, elle déposa la fraîcheur du scandale qui est la fraîcheur du vent matinal, l'étonnante douceur d'un bruit de sandale sur la pierre du temple . . .*" [In the big café with the closed windows drawn on their hollow rods, overcrowded and foundering in smoke, she wafted the coolness of a morning breeze, the astonishing sweetness of the sound of sandals on the stone of the temple . . .]. Here, in the first part of the sentence that describes Graff's, in terms that suggest heaviness and closure—"*baissé*" [closed], "*tiré*" [drawn], "*sombrant*" [foundering]—is the recurrent end syllable, the short, masculine and closed é, whereas Divine's effect is suggested with an alternation of the long, soft, open *eur* and *al*.

8. If one looks at the question in "coital" terms, it is true that they are the ones who are penetrated (unlike the straight cross-dressers, their phallus is never prominent). However—as I discuss in greater depth in the chapter on the phallus—Genet's work complicates the relationship that qualifies the penetrator as active and the penetrated as passive. The phallus does not invariably search for, pierce and enter flesh. Often it is still, inflexible and passive, and around it, the queens' bodies entwine themselves ["*s'entortillent*"] or over it they descend ["*s'enfilent*"].

9. Judith Butler, *Gender Trouble* (New York and London: Routledge, 1990), ix.

10. Oscar Montero, "Lipstick Vogue: The Politics of Drag," *Radical America* 22 (1989): 36–42.

11. Severo Sarduy, *Cobra*, trans. Suzanne Levine (Normal, IL: Dalkey Archives, 1995).

12. *Paris Is Burning* (Jenny Livingston, dir. and prod., Miramax, 1991), a film documentary about African-American and Hispanic drag queens in New York City, shows that gender differences are easier to overcome stylistically than differences of race or class. The feminine performances are superb and maintained both during and outside the competitive parades of the drag balls. Those categories such as "Businessman" or "Opulence" that demand an impersonation of "the Great White Way of Being," as one queen

puts it, function in a more carnivalesque fashion—that is, within the confines of the ball only and as a temporary fantasy fulfillment.

13. Introduction to *Fragments*, 17. I would argue, however, that Genet's suggestion of a certain heroism with which the homosexual lives his tragic flaw tempers this denunciation.

14. *Coming to Power*, ed. by members of SAMOIS, a lesbian feminist S/M organization (Boston: Alyson Publications, 1981).

15. Pat Califia, "Playing with Roles and Reversals: Gender Bending," *The Advocate* (September 1983): 24–26.

16. Ibid., 24.

17. The reference here is to the by now well known "masquerade" theory of femininity first put forth in 1929 by the psychoanalyst Joan Rivière in "Womanliness as a Masquerade." "The reader may now ask how I define womanliness or where I draw the line between genuine womanliness and the 'masquerade.' My suggestion is not, however, that there is any such difference; whether radical or superficial, they are the same thing." First published in *The International Journal of Psychoanalysis* 10 (1929). Reprinted in *Formations of Fantasy*, ed. Victor Burgin, James Donald, and Cora Kaplan (London: Methuen, 1986). See also Stephen Heath's essay in the same volume, "Joan Rivière and the Masquerade," and Judith Butler's discussion in *Gender Trouble*, 43–56.

18. Sue Ellen Case, "Towards a Butch/Femme Aesthetic," *Discourse* 11.1 (Fall–Winter 1998–1999): 55.

19. In fact, the fluctuations and reversals that gender-bending calls for ("the next time we see each other, I will probably be the one on my knees [...] the time after that we might both be men") are precisely meant to dissociate the roles more fully from the idea of an internal truth. Califia, "Playing with Roles," 43.

20. Wendy Chapkis, *Beauty Secrets: Women and the Politics of Appearance* (Boston: South End Press, 1986), 138.

21. Case, "Towards a Butch/Femme Aesthetic," 73.

22. There is no French term for camp.

23. Esther Newton, *Mother Camp: Female Impersonators in America* (Chicago: University of Chicago Press, 1979).

24. Ibid., 107.

25. Susan Sontag, "Notes on Camp," in *Against Interpretation* (New York: Octagon, 1982), 278–92.

26. Judith Butler, "Lana's 'Imitation': Melodramatic Repetition and the Gender Performative," *Genders* 9 (Fall 1990): 6.

27. "Remembering Stonewall," on *All Things Considered*, National Public Radio, 1 July 1989.

28. Newton, *Mother Camp*, 109. Newton also criticizes Sontag for almost editing homosexuals out of camp. Indeed, she makes the connection only

at the very end of the article and offers the astonishing opinion: "One feels that if homosexuals had not invented camp someone else would have."

29. Michael Bronski, *Culture Clash: The Making of a Gay Sensibility* (Boston: South End Press, 1984), 43.

30. This idea appears often in several of Cixous's texts: "The Laugh of the Medusa," "Castration or Decapitation?" *The Newly Born Woman.* See my earlier discussion of this in chapter 1.

31. As Toril Moi notes, this can be viewed as a rather essentializing moment in Cixous. See her *Sexual/Textual Politics: Feminist Literary Theory* (London and New York: Routledge, 1985), 110–11.

32. Verena Conley, *Hélène Cixous: Writing the Feminine* (Lincoln and London: University of Nebraska Press, 1984), 28.

33. Sandra Gilbert and Susan Gubar, *No Man's Land*, Vol. 2: *Sexchanges* (New Haven and London: Yale University Press, 1989), 324–76.

34. This seems to me a predominantly English or American trend. French cases seem more isolated. For the period Gilbert and Gubar discuss, only Colette comes to mind.

35. Gilbert and Gubar, *No Man's Land*, 331.

36. Virginia Woolf, *Orlando* (1928; New York: Harcourt Brace, 1973); Djuna Barnes, *Nightwood* (New York: Harcourt Brace, 1937).

37. Mary Jacobus, "Reading Woman (Reading)," in *Reading Woman*, ed. Mary Jacobus (New York: Columbia University Press, 1986), 4.

38. Gertrude Stein, *Tender Buttons* (New York: Claire Marie, 1914).

39. D. H. Lawrence, *Four Short Novels* (New York: Viking, 1968).

40. Ernest Hemingway, *The Garden of Eden* (New York: Scribner's, 1986).

41. James Joyce, *Ulysses* (New York: Random, 1934).

42. Gilbert and Gubar, *No Man's Land*, 333.

43. Ibid., 333–34.

44. Natalie Davis, *Society and Culture in Early Modern France* (Stanford, CA: Stanford University Press, 1975).

45. Elaine Showalter also relies on Stoller's analysis. She makes a connection between, on the one hand, the recent incursions of male academics into feminist discourse bolstered by their (tentative) claims that they might be able to read or write as women, and, on the other, the contemporary, mass-cultural fascination with female impersonators. Showalter considers the success of the movie *Tootsie* to be a manifestation of this fascination and argues that, rather than being a tribute to women, it shows and reasserts the triumph of masculine power behind feminine dress. Elaine Showalter, "Critical Cross-Dressing: Male Feminists and the Woman of the Year," in *Men in Feminism*, ed. Alice Jardine and Paul Smith, 116–33. (New York and London: Routledge, 1989).

46. According to Stoller, the cross-dresser's excitement comes from knowing that under the dress there is a penis. Marjorie Garber notes that

this hypothesis is clearly illustrated in practice: page after page of magazines for male transvestites depicts them "in panties, garter belts, maids' uniforms, boots and chains, each with naked, erect and prominently displayed cocks and balls." Marjorie Garber, *Vested Interests: Cross-Dressing and Cultural Anxiety* (New York and London: Routledge, 1992), 96.

47. Ibid.
48. Jacobus, *Reading Woman*, 4.
49. Marilyn Frye, "Lesbian Feminism and the Gay Rights Movement," in *The Politics of Reality* (Trumansburg, NY: Crossing Press, 1983), 128–50.
50. In *Paris Is Burning*, drag queen/pre-op transexual Octavia Saint-Laurent talks of her idol, supermodel Paulina Porizkova, in a tone of awed respect and deep affection, as she points to photographs: "I admire her so much . . . someday I hope to have my picture up there with hers . . . here she is so sexy and provocative . . . here she is so seductive and alluring . . . there she is more like a childish little girl."
51. Butler, *Gender Trouble*, 39.
52. Ibid., 132.
53. Ibid.

NOTES TO CHAPTER 2

1. Both *Saint Genet* and *The Second Sex* were published in 1952. The idea of women accepting unpleasant penetration to transcend their state of nonbeing pervades much of de Beauvoir's work. For example: "Shut up in the sphere of the relative, destined to the male from childhood, habituated to seeing in him a superb being whom she cannot possibly equal, the woman who has not repressed her claim to humanity will dream of transcending her being toward one of these superior beings, of amalgamating herself with the sovereign subject" Simone de Beauvoir, *The Second Sex*, trans. H. M. Parshley (New York; Knopf, 1953), 113.
2. For the time being, I am remaining within the conventional definitions of activity and passivity.
3. Kaja Silverman, *Male Subjectivity at the Margins* (New York: Routledge, 1992), 355.
4. Leo Bersani, "Is the Rectum a Grave," *October* 43 (1987): 197–216.
5. Altman, *The Homosexualization of America*, 213.
6. However, in the same manner as, in the previous chapter, I warned against the idealized notions of agency, consent, and choice, I will guard against the belief in a utopic erotic space where all desires are encouraged to proliferate and meet endless bounty and generosity.
7. Kate Millett, *Sexual Politics* (New York: Simon and Schuster, 1969), 340.

8. I do not want to suggest that the males, in Genet, are reduced to raw flesh—for he does draw attention to their particular way of moving, as we have seen, of talking, of dressing. But Genet makes it quite clear that this style is enabled by and a reflection of their anatomy. It is a birth privilege: "The only ones who could speak slang were the men who at birth received as a gift the gestures, the carriage of the hips, legs and arms, the chest with which one can speak it" (*OLF*, 99).

9. Marcel Proust, *Remembrance of Things Past*, trans. C. K. Scott Moncrief and Terence Kilmartin (New York: Vintage, 1982).

10. To be fair to Sartre, one should note that he does recognize the motif of the flowering penis but does not draw any conclusions from it.

11. The motif of the veiled body, whereby cloth suggests what it conceals, is a familiar one in the erotics of the female body.

12. Jacques Lacan, "The Signification of the Phallus," in *Ecrits: A Selection*, trans. Alan Sheridan, 281–91 (New York: Norton, 1977), 288.

13. Kaja Silverman, "The Lacanian Phallus," *Differences* 4.1 (1992): 85–116.

14. Ibid., 88.

15. Ibid., 89.

Notes to Chapter 3

1. White, *Jean Genet*, 503.

2. For a fascinating and lively account of this visit and of Genet's notoriety in the U.S. see Ibid., 506–14.

3. Ibid., 515

4. This notion, "to endow the Black race with form," is particularly interesting and opens up the question of the relationship of form to identity, which will be explored further in this chapter.

5. Quoted by White, *Jean Genet*, 481.

6. White, *Jean Genet*, 439.

7. Quoted by White, *Jean Genet*, 432.

8. Ibid., 132.

9. White, *Jean Genet*, 211.

10. Bobby Seale, "Selections from the Biography of Huey P. Newton," 21–34, *Ramparts* 15–30 (October 1968), 52.

11. George Jackson joined the Black Panther Party in 1966 while serving a prison sentence, which extended over ten years, often in solitary confinement, for driving the getaway car in a petty theft of $70. Edmund White succinctly described the events that, in January 1970, brought Jackson to national attention:

> Although racial antagonism ran high among the prisoners at Soledad, the authorities opened a new exercise yard on 13 January

1970, placed in it ten whites and seven Blacks. When a fight broke
out, predictably enough between the Blacks and whites, a guard
fired on them, killing three Blacks and wounding a white. A local
grand jury found that it had been an act of justifiable homicide.
Half an hour after the verdict was broadcast over the radio, a white
guard was found dead—thrown from the balcony onto the ground
below. Three Black political leaders in the prison, including
George Jackson, were accused of killing the guard. These three
were the "Soledad Brothers." (White, *Jean Genet*, 310)

To draw attention to Jackon's cause, his lawyers planned to publish his
prison letters and asked Genet to write the introduction. Genet enthusiasti-
cally agreed. But further tragedy occurred when, in August 1970, George's
brother Jonathan was killed after entering the trial of another San Quentin
prisoner with concealed weapons and taking the District Attorney, judge
and three jurors as hostages, with the intention of exchanging them for the
Soledad Brothers. Angela Davis, a friend of George and Jonathan, was accused of being an accomplice in this matter and was listed by the FBI as one
of the ten most wanted people in the United States. Genet, who had met
her and held her in great esteem, wrote several appeals on her behalf and
even enlisted Sartre's aid in her defense. On August 21, 1971, two days before his trial was scheduled to begin, George Jackson was killed in San
Quentin.

NOTES TO CHAPTER 4

1. Edward Said, "On Jean Genet's Late Works," 24–42, *Grand Street* 9.4
(Summer 1990), 38. Said wrote this in 1990. The Israeli-Palestinian rapprochement that has occurred since then might alter this statement somewhat.
    2. Ibid., 34.
    3. Ibid.
    4. Ibid.
    5. Ibid.

NOTES TO CONCLUSION

1. Catherine Millot, *Gide, Genet, Mishima: l'intelligence de la perversion*
(Paris: Gallimard, 1996).
    2. Ibid., 9.
    3. Leo Bersani, *Homos* (Cambridge: Harvard University Press, 1995),
173.
    4. Marie Redonnet, *Jean Genet: le poète travesti: portrait d'une oeuvre*
(Paris: B. Grasset, 2000).

5. Ibid., 237.

6. Marie-Claude Hubert, *L'Esthétique de Jean Genet* (Paris: SEDES, 1996).

7. Jean Genet, *Rembrandt*, trans. Randolph Hough (New York: Hanuman Books, 1988).

8. Félix Guattari, "Genet retrouvé," *Journal d'études Palestiniennes,* Hors série, Spring 1997.

9. Ibid,. 54.

10. Bersani, *Homos*, 7.

11. Ibid.

12. Guattari, "Genet retrouvé," 50.

13. Denis Hollier, *The Politics of Prose: Essay on Sartre*, trans. Jeffrey Mehlman (Minneapolis: University of Minnesota Press, 1986).

14. Susan Sontag, "Fascinating Fascism," in *Under the Sign of Saturn* (New York: Farrar, Strauss, Giroux, 1980).

15. Quoted in White, *Jean Genet*, 73.

16. Bersani, *Homos*, 167.

17. Ibid., 168.

18. Genet/Fichte Interview, 38.

19. Hadrien Laroche, *Le Dernier Genet: histoire des hommes infâmes* (Paris: Seuil, 1997), 171.

20. Ibid.

Bibliography

Altman, Dennis. *The Homosexualization of America: the Americanization of the Homosexual.* New York: St. Martin's Press, 1982.

Aslan, Odette. *Jean Genet.* Paris: Seghers, 1973.

Barnes, Djuna. *Nightwood.* New York: Harcourt Brace, 1937.

Bersani, Leo. *Homos.* Cambridge: Harvard University Press, 1995.

———. "Is the Rectum a Grave?" *October* 43 (1987): 197–216.

Bickel, Gisèle A. Child. *Jean Genet: criminalité et transcendance.* Saratoga, CA: Anma Libri, 1987.

Bonnefoy, Claude. *Jean Genet . . .* Paris: Éditions Universitaires, 1965.

Bronski, Michael. *Culture Clash: The Making of a Gay Sensibility.* Boston: South End Press, 1984.

Butler, Judith. *Gender Trouble.* New York and London: Routledge, 1990.

———. "Lana's 'Imitation': Melodramatic Repetition and the Gender Performative." *Genders* 9 (Fall 1990): 1–18.

Califia, Pat. "Playing with Roles and Reversals: Gender Bending." *The Advocate* (September 1983): 24–26.

Case, Sue Ellen. "Towards a Butch/Femme Aesthetic." *Discourse* 11.1 (Fall–Winter 1998–1999): 55–73.

Chapkis, Wendy. *Beauty Secrets: Women and the Politics of Appearance.* Boston: South End Press, 1986.

Cixous, Hélène. "Castration or Decapitation?" *Signs* 7.1 (1981): 41–55.

———. "The Laugh of the Medusa." Translated by Keith Cohen and Paula Cohen. *Signs* 1 (Summer 1976): 245–66.

Cixous, Hélène, and Catherine Clément. *The Newly Born Woman,* trans. Betsy Wing. Minneapolis: University of Minnesota Press, 1986.

Conley, Verena. *Hélène Cixous: Writing the Feminine.* Lincoln and London: University of Nebraska Press, 1984.

Davis, Natalie. *Society and Culture in Early Modern France.* Stanford, CA: Stanford University Press, 1975.

de Beauvoir, Simone. *La Cérémonie des adieux.* Paris: Gallimard, 1981.

———. *La Force de l'âge.* Paris: Gallimard, 1960.

———. *The Second Sex,* trans. H. M. Parshley. New York: Knopf, 1953.

Derrida, Jacques. *Dissemination,* trans. Barbara Johnson. London: Athlone Press, 1981.

———. *Glas. English,* trans. John P, Leavey, Jr. and Richard Rand. Lincoln and London: University of Nebraska Press, 1986.

El Basri, Aïcha. *L'Imaginaire carcéral de Jean Genet.* Paris: L'Harmattan, 1999.

Fredette, Nathalie. *Figures baroques de Jean Genet.* Montréal: XYZ; Saint-Denis: Presses Universitaries de Vincennes, 2001.

Frye, Marilyn. "Lesbian Feminism and the Gay Rights Movement." In *The Politics of Reality,* 128–50. Trumansburg, NY: Crossing Press, 1983.

Gaitet, Pascale. *Political Stylistics.* New York: Routledge, 1992.

Garber, Marjorie. *Vested Interests: Cross-Dressing and Cultural Anxiety.* New York and London: Routledge, 1992.

Genet, Jean. *Chants secrets.* Décines: L'Arbalète, 1945.

———. "Fragments." In *Fragments . . . et autres textes,* 69–97. Paris: Gallimard, 1990.

———. *Funeral Rites,* trans. Bernard Frechtman. New York: Grove Press, 1969.

———. Interview by Hubert Fichte. Frankfurt and Paris: Qumran Verlag, 1981.

———. *L'Ennemi déclaré.* Paris: Gallimard, 1991.

———. *Miracle of the Rose,* trans. Bernard Frechtman. New York: Grove, 1967.

———. *Our Lady of the Flowers,* trans. Bernard Frechtman. New York: Grove, 1987.

———. *Prisoner of Love,* trans. Barbara Bray. Hanover: Wesleyan University Press, 1992.

———. *Querelle,* trans. Anselm Hollo. First Evergreen Edition. New York: Grove/Weidenfeld, 1987.

———. *Rembrandt,* trans. Randolph Hough (New York: Hanuman Books, 1988).

———. *The Blacks,* trans. Bernard Frechtman. New York: Grove Press, 1960.

———. *The Maids,* trans. Bernard Frechtman. New York: Grove Press, 1954.

———. *The Screens,* trans. Bernard Frechtman. New York: Grove Press, 1963.

———. *The Thief's Journal,* trans. Bernard Frechtman. New York: Grove Press, 1973.

Gilbert, Sandra, and Susan Gubar. *No Man's Land,* Vol. 2: *Sexchanges.* New Haven and London: Yale University Press, 1989.

Gluck, Robert. *Jack the Modernist.* New York: Gay Presses of New York, 1995.

Guattari, Félix. "Genet retrouvé." *Journal d'études Palestiniennes.* Hors série (Spring 1997).

Hanrahan, Mairéad. *Lire Genet: une poétique de la différence.* Montréal: Presses de l'Université de Montréal, 1997.

Heath, Stephen. "Joan Rivière and the Masquerade." In *Formations of Fantasy,* ed. Victor Burgin, James Donald, and Cora Kaplan, 45–61. London: Methuen, 1986.

Hemingway, Ernest. *The Garden of Eden.* New York: Scribner's, 1986.

Hollier, Denis. *The Politics of Prose: Essay on Sartre,* trans. Jeffrey Mehlman. Minneapolis: University of Minnesota Press, 1986.

Hubert, Marie-Claude. *L'Esthétique de Jean Genet.* Paris: SEDES, 1996.

Jackson, George. *Soledad Brother: The Prison Letters of George Jackson.* New York: Coward-McCann, 1970.

Jacobus, Mary. "Reading Woman (Reading)." In *Reading Woman,* ed. Mary Jacobus, 3–24. New York: Columbia University Press, 1986.

Joyce, James. *Ulysses.* New York: Random, 1934.

Knapp, Bettina Liebowitz. *Jean Genet.* Rev. ed. Boston: Twayne, 1989.

Kristeva, Julia. *Revolution in Poetic Language,* trans. Margaret Waller. New York: Columbia University Press, 1984.

Lacan, Jacques. "The Signification of the Phallus." In *Ecrits: A Selection,* trans. Alan Sheridan, 281–91. New York: Norton, 1977.

Laroche, Hadrien. *Le Dernier Genet: histoire des hommes infâmes.* Paris: Seuil, 1997.

Lawrence, D. H. *Four Short Novels.* New York: Viking, 1968.

Livingston, Jenny, dir. and prod. *Paris Is Burning.* Miramax Films, 1991.

Magnan, Jean Marie. *Jean Genet.* Paris: P. Seghers, 1966.

Marchand, Alain Bernard. *Genet le joueur impénitent: essai.* Montréal: Les Herbes Rouges, 1997.

McMahon, Joseph H. *The Imagination of Jean Genet.* New Haven: Yale University Press, 1963.

Millett, Kate. *Sexual Politics.* New York: Simon and Schuster, 1969.

Millot, Catherine. *Gide, Genet, Mishima: l'intelligence de la perversion.* Paris: Gallimard, 1996.

Moi, Toril. *Sexual/Textual Politics: Feminist Literary Theory.* London and New York: Routledge, 1985.

Montero, Oscar. "Lipstick Vogue: The Politics of Drag." *Radical America* 22 (1989): 36–42.

Moraly, Jean-Bernard. *Jean Genet: le vie écrite.* Paris: Éditions de la Différence, 1988.

Naish, Camille. *A Genetic Approach to Structures in the Work of Jean Genet.* Cambridge: Harvard University Press, Department of Romance Languages and Literatures, 1978.

Newton, Esther. *Mother Camp: Female Impersonators in America.* Chicago: University of Chicago Press, 1979.

Oswald, Laura. *Jean Genet and the Semiotics of Performance.* Bloomington: Indiana University Press, 1989.

Proust, Marcel. *Remembrance of Things Past,* trans. C. K. Scott Moncrief and Terence Kilmartin. New York: Vintage, 1982.

Redonnet, Marie. *Jean Genet, le poète travesti: portrait d'une ouvre.* Paris: B. Grasset, 2000.

Rivière, Joan. "Womanliness as a Masquerade." In *The International Journal of Psychoanalysis* 10 (1929). Reprinted in *Formations of Fantasy,* ed. Victor Burgin, James Donald, and Cora Kaplan, 35–44. London: Methuen, 1986.

Ross, Andrew. *Universal Abandon.* Minneapolis: University of Minnesota Press, 1988.

Said, Edward. "On Jean Genet's Late Works." *Grand Street* 9.4 (Summer 1990): 24–42.

SAMOIS. *Coming to Power: Writings and Graphics on Lesbian S/M,* ed. by members of SAMOIS. Boston: Alyson Publications, 1981.

Sarduy, Severo. *Cobra,* trans. Suzanne Levine. Norma, Illinois: Dalkey Archives, 1995.

Sartre, Jean-Paul. *Roads to Freedom,* trans. Eric Sutton. New York: Knopf, 1959.

———. *Saint Genet: Actor and Martyr,* trans. Bernard Frechtman. New York: George Braziller, 1963.

———. *Search for a Method,* trans. Hazel Barnes. New York: Knopf, 1963.

———. *The Age of Reason,* trans. Eric Sutton. New York: Knopf, 1966.

Seale, Bobby. "Selections from the Biography of Huey P. Newton." *Ramparts* 15–30 (October 1968): 21–34.

Showalter, Elaine. "Critical Cross-Dressing: Male Feminists and the Woman of the Year." In *Men in Feminism,* ed. Alice Jardine and Paul Smith, 116–33. New York and London: Routledge, 1989.

Shukri, Muhammad. *Jean Genet in Tangier,* trans. Paul Bowles. Introduction by William Burroughs. New York: Ecco Press, 1974.

Silverman, Kaja. *Male Subjectivity at the Margins.* New York: Routledge, 1992.

———. "The Lacanian Phallus." *Differences* 4.1 (1992): 85–116.

Sontag, Susan. "Fascinating Fascism." In *Under the Sign of Saturn,* 82–113. New York: Farrar, Strauss, Giroux, 1980.

———. "Notes on Camp." In *Against Interpretation,* 278–92. New York: Octagon, 1982.

Stein, Gertrude. *Tender Buttons*. New York: Claire Marie, 1914.

Thody, Philip Malcolm Waller. *Jean Genet: A Study of His Novels and Plays*. London: H. Hamilton, 1968.

White, Edmund. *Jean Genet: A Biography*. New York: Knopf, 1993.

Woolf, Virginia. *Orlando*. New York: Harcourt Brace, 1928, 1973.

Index